MAKA[R]

WALKS IN THE OLD TOWN OF EDIN[BURGH]
WITH *AN ANTHOLOGY OF POETRY*

Selected and Walked by Duncan Glen

ANTHOLOGY

Edinburgh
THE SCOTTISH POETRY LIBRARY
&
EDINBURGH
OLD TOWN TRUST
1990

First published 1990
by The Scottish Poetry Library
Tweeddale Court, 14 High Street, Edinburgh
with
Edinburgh Old Town Trust
Advocate's Close, 357 High Street, Edinburgh
Text, selection, and notes
© copyright Duncan Glen 1990
© copyright of poems remains with
the authors or their executors

Typeset by Paul Conkie
at Scotland's Cultural Heritage, Edinburgh
Printed in Scotland by Pace Print, Edinburgh
Bound by Hunter & Foulis, Edinburgh

9|11|90

ACKNOWLEDGEMENTS

First I have to thank Tessa Ransford who saw my presentation of a reading, for three voices and a singer, entitled "Heich and Laich" at the Poetry Association of Scotland and commissioned me to do the original performance of this "Makars' Walk" for the Old Town Gala of 1989. I have to thank Margaret Bennett, Martyn Bennett, Donald Campbell, Irene McFarlane and Ken Nelson for making that performance one that captured a large audience in Tweeddale Court. I have to thank the Old Town Trust and The Scottish Poetry Library for encouraging me to turn that performance into a book. As always I am indebted to the Scottish Poetry Library, the Scottish Room and the Edinburgh Room of Edinburgh Central Public Library and the National Library of Scotland for assistance. I am grateful to Mr John Mitchell for scholarly advice on the buildings of the High School. Mr Ian Begg gave quiet but influential advice. To Mr R. W. Smith I am grateful not only for help in researching the illustrations but for a scholarly and enthusiastic response to both the Walks and the texts of the poems. My thanks to Mr Alfons Bytautas for introducing me to the etchings of Walter Geikie and to Mrs Anne Morrison of Edinburgh City Libraries for help in tracing Geikie's work. I am grateful to Rev. A. Sinclair Horne of the Scottish Reformation Society for help not only in finding illustrations but with the reproduction of them. I thank Mr Paul Conkie for his patience and care in following my design in typesetting and formatting the text. My thanks to all those, of many nationalities, whom I met and who responded with enthusiasm to match my own as I was making these Makars' Walks. As always I am indebted to my wife for assisting with copy preparation and indicating to me where I was failing to communicate as I intended.

For permission to print poems the publishers make acknowledgement to: the executors of Marion Angus, to Donald Campbell, Douglas Fraser, the executors of Robert Garioch and Macdonald Publishers, to Duncan Glen, Tom Hubbard, Alexander Hutchison, Norman MacCaig and Chatto & Windus, to the executors of Hugh MacDiarmid, to Forbes Macgregor, to the executors of John W. Oliver, to Walter Perrie, Tessa Ransford, to the executors of Alexander Scott, the executors of Sydney Goodsir Smith and John Calder (Publishers) Ltd, and the executors of Lewis Spence. For permission to print the music to "Blackfriars Wynd" acknowledgement is made to Robert Pettigrew. The drawing of Robert Fergusson is printed by kind permission of the Trustees of the National Library of Scotland from the Cape papers. The portrait of Fergusson by Runciman is printed by kind permission of the National Galleries of Scotland as is the silhouette of Clarinda. The cover drawing and the etchings by Walter Geikie are reproduced by courtesy of Edinburgh City Libraries.

3

CONTENTS

NIGHT LIFE

LOVE

SATIRE AND CHARACTERS

THE CITY WE LIVE IN

Robert Fergusson

The Netherbow Port

WALK 1
FROM HOLYROOD TO ST GILES

James IV

Margaret Tudor

The backbone of the Old Town of Edinburgh is the Royal Mile which comprises four continuous streets - Castlehill, Lawnmarket, High Street and Canongate. In the early years of the eighteenth century Daniel Defoe wrote of this Royal Mile as "perhaps the largest, longest and finest Street for Buildings and Number of Inhabitants, not in *Britain* only, but in the world".

This first Makars' Walk begins at the foot of the Canongate. We start in Abbey Strand by a heraldic panel set into the wall near the gates of the Palace of Holyroodhouse. It bears the Royal Arms and I R 5 for King James the Fifth who is the first poet of this Makars' Walk. His ancestor James I wrote considerably greater poetry being almost certainly the author of *The Kingis Quair* written in 1435. Whether James I or James V wrote the influential poem "Christ's Kirk on the Green" will never be resolved but the form of the poem was a popular one into this century and that the debate should be over royal authorship says something that can only be creditable to these Kings of Scots.

Leaving the heraldic panel of the time of James V we go through into the forecourt of the Palace of Holyroodhouse. To left and right are the very fine wrought iron gates which are part of a memorial to Edward VII which was erected in the early 1920's. The tower facing us to the left-hand side was built for James V in 1529-32 but the present-day Palace is predominantly that built for Charles II.

Behind the Palace are the ruins of the Abbey of Holy Rood which was founded by David I in 1128; canons of the Order of St Augustine were given control of it and so the road from the Abbey to the Netherbow became known as the Canongate - the canon's way or road. On Castle Rock at the other end of the Royal Mile within the Castle is Saint Margaret's Chapel, the oldest building in Edinburgh. The popular belief was that Malcolm III built this chapel for Queen Margaret, his pious second wife, but it is now accepted that her son David I built it and dedicated it to his mother. Queen Margaret died in the Castle in 1093 and the notice outside her chapel in Edinburgh Castle informs that she was created a saint in 1251. For a response to this chapel see my poem on page 75.

For centuries the poets of Edinburgh were poets of the Stewart court and the greatest of them is William Dunbar. His poetry gives us a unique insight into the court of James IV in Edinburgh in the late fifteenth and early sixteenth centuries and in his poem "To the Merchantis of Edinburgh" we get a picture of the High Street of Edinburgh of that time, even if it is a satirical and unflattering one - see page 72. We can, however, recognise aspects of Edinburgh that were to survive for centuries and some to this day. The "parroche kirk" is St Giles, the "High Croce" has moved but, in another form, is there today. The "stinkand style" was a passage through the Luckenbooths which were on the High Street for centuries, see Walk 3. The "principall gaittis" were in the town wall and remnants of town walls feature in the walks of this book.

If we imagine William Dunbar walking the High Street of Edinburgh in the late fifteenth century we would see him writing poems which were very much part of the ceremonial of James IV's court. At least three of Dunbar's poems must have graced the festivities of the wedding of the King and Margaret Tudor, daughter of Henry VII of England and sister of Henry VIII. The wedding took place on 8th August 1503 in the Abbey Church of Holyrood, the bride being not yet fourteen.

A near contemporary of William Dunbar was Gavin Douglas, son of the fifth Earl of Angus who was picturesquely nicknamed "Bell-the-Cat" although he earned this soubriquet by an act of extreme violence. The poet was no more squeamish than his father. As a Douglas, Gavin the poet was, for a time after the death of James IV at the Battle of Flodden, in a far more powerful position at court than Dunbar who never received the preferment he sought, not that everyone regarded these Red Douglases with sympathetic eyes. One such observer was to write "all the court was rewlit (ruled) by the Erle of Angus, Mr Gawin Douglas, and the Drummonds - bot nocht weill".

Gavin Douglas's greatest work was his translation of Virgil's *Aeneid* which he completed only weeks before the defeat of the Scots at the battle of Flodden on 9th September 1513. The great lament for this defeat is the song "The Flowers of the Forest" versions of which were written by several poets including Alison Cockburn whose grave is on the route of Walk 2.

Mary Queen of Scots

In the memories of visitors to Holyroodhouse the name of Mary Queen of Scots no doubt lingers longest, see the poems on pages 42 - 47. Her favourite David Rizzio was murdered in the Palace in 1566. See Norman MacCaig's poem on, amongst other realities, the realities of Mary and Rizzio on page 46. What followed for Mary, and Darnley and Bothwell her husbands, was a succession of not only state but personal tragedies, resulting finally in her abdication on 24th July 1567 in favour of her son James VI. Mary's court, although a troubled one, was alive with song and music. The poets had welcomed her back, including Alexander Scott who was both poet and musician and perhaps the greatest Scottish love poet before Robert Burns. See his poems on pages 47 and 68.

Even as a boy-King James VI was a more clever politician than his mother. When Elizabeth of England died in 1603 James succeeded to the English throne and immediately left Scotland for London, thereby removing the patronage of a resident court from the Scottish poets. James made only one return visit to his Scottish capital, in May 1617, although before he went south he had promised a large congregation in St Giles' Church that he would return to his capital every three years. Before he left Edinburgh, however, James had encouraged a revival of a distinctively Scottish poetry although, as always, with European ideas absorbed into the native tradition. James himself wrote poetry, as did his mother, Mary, his grandfather James V, and his ancestor James I, the greatest of Scotland's royal poets. A sonnet by James VI is printed on page 48.

William Drummond

The "maister poete" of James VI was Alexander Montgomerie, although he was to become involved in Catholic intrigue and so lose the King's favour. The poem by Montgomerie on page 48 is addressed to Robert Hudson who was also at the court of James VI and indeed succeeded Montgomerie as "maister poete"; in the poem Montgomerie may be asking Fowler to intercede with the King on his behalf.

For James VI's visit to Edinburgh William Drummond wrote a poem to be read on the King's arrival and also another entitled "Forth Feasting: a Panegyricke to the King's Most Excellent Majesty", see page 47. The Scottish Parliament was less

Allan Ramsay

Clarinda

JAMES BURNET,
Lord Monboddo,
One of his Majesty's Judges of
the Court of Session in Scotland.

pleased with the King whose aim was to impose the Anglican service and form of church government on Scotland. Fortunately he had sense enough to back down.

We leave the Palace of Holyroodhouse, passing the statue of Edward VII, by the grand gates to the north of the statue. Over to the left stands a small strange building. It is called Queen Mary's Bathhouse and is the subject of the poem by Lewis Spence on page 46; it is mentioned by Sydney Goodsir Smith in his poem printed on page 73, although the purpose of this fantasy of a building remains a mystery.

We turn left along Abbeyhill to come to Calton Road and looking up it the large monument to Robert Burns can be seen. We cross into Canongate and come to White Horse Close. On a fine old and restored house a plaque informs us that this is the site of White Horse Inn, see poem by Forbes Macgregor on page 64. Past Whitefoord House we come to a plaque which refers to Walter Scott's novel *The Abbot*. Across the road is Queensberry House, see Forbes Macgregor's poem on page 64. We continue uphill to the site of Jenny Ha's Change House which was a tavern where the eighteenth-century Edinburgh poet Allan Ramsay drank with convivial friends. We pass the modern pub of that name, Clarinda's tearoom, a plaque indicating the whereabouts of Panmure House where Adam Smith spent his last years, to come to no.137 Canongate, or Dunbar's Close. Going through the Close we enter the peaceful Dunbar's Close Garden which is laid out in the style of a seventeenth-century Edinburgh garden. The Close and Garden are named after David Dunbar who owned property here in the eighteenth century and not the poet William Dunbar but this is a pleasant place to sit and think of his work, including his great poem "The Tretis of the Twa Mariit Wemen and the Wedo" in which these uninhibited women talk as they sit in a green garden. Again on the skyline the Burns m0ument can be seen; it is by Thomas Hamilton (1830).

Leaving that pleasant garden we come in a few yards to Canongate Kirk and Kirkyard; the Kirk being beautiful in its simplicity. Following the path to the left of it we come in a few yards to a short path with red chipstones leading to the grave of the poet Robert Fergusson who was to Edinburgh in the eighteenth century what in their times Villon was to Paris, Dickens to London and James Joyce to Dublin. The headstone on Fergusson's grave was erected by Robert Burns who wrote the epitaph it bears, see page 53. On the back of the stone is an inscription written by Burns. The twentieth-century Edinburgh poet Robert Garioch, who felt an affinity with Fergusson, wrote a poem entitled "At Robert Fergusson's Grave" see page 53, and extracts from his poem "To Robert Fergusson" are printed on page 54.

From Fergusson's grave we take the path to the left of the church. Again we can see the Burns m0ument and on the wall at the end of the path there is a memorial with a golden head. Beneath that portrait is one word CLARINDA. It is the grave of Mrs McLehose who exchanged famous love letters with Robert Burns and to whom he sent one of his greatest love songs, "Ae Fond Kiss", see page 70.

Leaving Canongate Kirkyard we continue uphill under the Canongate Tolbooth clock where we cross the street and pass a gateway with pointed pillars to come to the entrance to St John's Street, or Pend, where a plaque tells us that the novelist Smollett occasionally lived here. Here also lived the eccentric Lord Monboddo and his daughter Elizabeth Burnet, immortalised as "Fair Burnet strikes th' adorin' eye" in Burns's poem "Address to Edinburgh". This might seem a poem suitable for this book but, sadly, the above is a good line in a very bad poem. In St John's Street are also the premises of Canongate Kilwinning Masonic Lodge to which, popular tradition says, Burns was appointed Poet Laureate. A few yards uphill is a painted cross in the road which marks the spot where stood the standing cross of St John on the boundary between Edinburgh and the burgh of Canongate.

We continue up Canongate to the traffic lights with St Mary's Street on the left and Jeffrey Street on the right. Down St Mary's Street on the left was Boyd's Inn to which Samuel Johnston came before beginning his tour of the Hebrides. When Johnston left Boyd's Inn he went to James Boswell's rooms in the Royal Mile, in James's Court where David Hume the philosopher had also lived. For a juxtaposition of Hume and Boswell see Alexander Hutchison's poem on page 82.

One of the results of the defeat of the Scots at the Battle of Flodden in 1513 was that the citizens of Edinburgh, fearing an advance northwards by the victorious English, built a new wall around their town, known as the Flodden Wall. The city within that wall comprised less than 140 acres and so can be walked from end to end in only a few minutes, although if you follow the routes of my literary walks it will take somewhat longer. A wall earlier than Flodden is known as the King's Wall; it was built in the middle of the fifteenth century on the authority of James II. In his poem "To the Merchantis of Edinburgh" William Dunbar refers to the gates in the wall which gave access to the city, see page 72.

The eastern part of the Flodden Wall ran along the line of today's St Mary's Street. For those who wish to follow the route of the Flodden Wall it is, in terms of today's streets, down St Mary's Street, along the Pleasance, Drummond Street, South College Street, Bristo Port, Bristo Place, Teviot Place, Lauriston Place, Heriot Place, the Vennel and the west end of the Grassmarket. I take this route from Lord Cullen's *The Walls of Edinburgh,* see further reading list on page 84.

At this historic point, where Canongate meets High Street in the Flodden Wall, was the Netherbow Port, or gate, which gave access from Edinburgh into the outside world. It is not for nothing that, a few yards from here, the last close in the High Street is named World's End Close. There are brass markings set into the road to indicate where the Netherbow Port stood. One rectangle seems to remain particularly unworn, perhaps to remind those of us who would over-confidently date past events of our fallibility; within that rectangle is —"?1514".

An idea of what the Netherbow Port looked like can be had from an impression of it cut in stone above no. 9 High Street and from the bronze sculptural impression of it which hangs outside the Netherbow Centre of the Church of Scotland a few yards up from no. 9. Inside the entrance to the Centre is the seventeenth-century bell of the Port and through in the courtyard is a plaque taken from the Port which is dated 1606 and bears the initials of James VI.

The Netherbow Port was demolished in 1764 to facilitate the flow of traffic but this is a spot that features often in the poetry of this book and if it was an escape to Canongate pubs for Allan Ramsay and his literary friends, see poem on page 56, it was also an entry into Edinburgh for Kings and Queens. Mary passed through it on her ceremonial return to Edinburgh from France and it was through a newly-repaired Netherbow that James VI entered the city in 1617. As Walter Scott wrote in his masterpiece on Edinburgh, *The Heart of Midlothian,* "The Netherbow Port might be called the Temple Bar of Edinburgh, it divided Edinburgh from the Canongate, as

A

TREATISE

OF

Human Nature:

BEING

An ATTEMPT to introduce the experimental Method of Reasoning

INTO

MORAL SUBJECTS.

Rara temporum felicitas, ubi sentire, quæ velis; & quæ sentias, dicere licet. TACIT.

VOL. I.

OF THE

UNDERSTANDING.

LONDON:

Printed for JOHN NOON, at the *White-Hart,* near *Mercer's-Chapel,* in *Cheapside.*

MDCCXXXIX.

David Hume's masterpiece

James Boswell

Portrait of Allan Ramsay from 1721-28 two-volume edition of his poems

Temple Bar separates London from Westminster".

We cross from the Netherbow Centre to Tweeddale Court, home, most appropriately, of the Scottish Poetry Library. The Library is approached through the arch of a stylish wrought-iron gate and to the right is a wall, thought to be one of the few surviving parts of the old King's Wall which preceded the Flodden Wall. Also on the right is what is thought to have been a shed for sedan chairs. The Poetry Library was created by Tessa Ransford, its Director. Its Librarian is Tom Hubbard whose poem on Tweeddale Court is printed on page 78. Tessa Ransford also has written poems of Edinburgh, see pages 39, 82 and 83. For another poem on Tweeddale Court see that by John W. Oliver on page 78 which is on Oliver & Boyd, the publishers, whose name remains above their old premises although they have been long gone from the Court.

Tweeddale Court

Leaving the Poetry Library we cross the road to John Knox House. Knox was the arch enemy of Mary Queen of Scots and he used his *History of the Reformation* to attack her and the goings-on at her artistic and musical court. In his *History* he writes of the year 1563, "At the very time of the General Assembly, there comes to public knowledge a heinous crime committed in the Court, yea, not far from the Queen's own lap; for a French woman, that served in the Queen's chamber had played the whore with the Queen's own apothecary. The woman conceived and bore a child, whom with common consent the father and the mother murdered. Yet were the cries of a new born bairn heard; search was made, the child and mother were both deprehended: and so were both the man and the woman damned to be hanged upon the public street of Edinburgh". This is propaganda against Catholic Mary; Knox also refers to another affair in which "shame hastened marriage betwixt John Sempell, called the Dancer, and Marie Livingstone, surnamed the Lusty. What bruit the Maries and the rest of the dancers of the Court had, the ballads of that age did witness, which we may with modesty omit". Sadly these ballads do not seem to have survived. This Marie Livingstone was one of the four Maries who accompanied the child Queen to France in 1548. A daughter of Lord Livingstone, she married John Sempill, a natural son of Lord Sempill, but Knox libelled them in his phrase, "shame hastened marriage".

We may not have the ballads referred to by Knox but we have the ballad of "Marie Hamilton" in which the maid has become Marie Hamilton and the apothecary Mary's husband Darnley, although by Knox's dating of his story Darnley was nowhere near Edinburgh at the crucial time. Not that this is important to the art-form that is the ballad. The four high-born Maries who accompanied Queen Mary to France were Marie Livingstone, Marie Fleming, Marie Seaton and Marie Beaton. Again, as is the way with ballads, the names have been changed, and differently in one version from another.

For the version of "Marie Hamilton" printed on pages 44-5 I have cobbled together verses taken from Charles Kirkpatrick Sharpe and Walter Scott. Most of the places named in the ballad have been mentioned in this walk already, the court and the abbey were at Holyrood and so to go up the Canongate was to go to the separate town, or burgh, of Edinburgh through the Netherbow Port to the law court in the Tolbooth and finally to the gallows at the Mercat Cross. Later in this walk we will come to the site of the Tolbooth by St Giles and in Walk 2 to Kirk o' Field, where Darnley was murdered. Darnley is another court poet and for his poem "To the Queen" see page 42.

John Knox

The Tron Kirk

Leaving John Knox House we move past a pub which has a silver portrait of the poet Allan Ramsay on display, to Carrubers Close where Allan Ramsay attempted to establish a theatre only to have it closed down by the authorities. His comedians took sanctuary in Holyrood. If we go down Carrubers Close we come to Old St Paul's Episcopal Church where we may hear beautiful music, as did Alexander Hutchison. See page 69 for his poem "Fleurs-de Lys".

Here on the High Street facing today's Niddry Street was Allan Ramsay's first bookshop. At the traffic lights at North and South Bridges we cross to the Tron Kirk. This fine old church stood empty for many years but now it is being used to encourage the continuing revitalisation of the Old Town. The Tron Kirk was built at the instigation of Charles I but he had to insist before the city fathers would carry out his wishes as, although the foundation of this Christ's Kirk at the Tron was laid in 1637, it did not open for worship until 1647. The Kirk has a fine oak roof with an unusual latticed truss construction which was probably erected by the same craftsmen who worked on the roof of Parliament Hall. The bell of the Tron Kirk was addressed in a poem by Robert Fergusson, see page 79, but the one which aroused the poet's fury was replaced in 1774; today the bell is silent even when crowds gather by the Kirk to see in the New Year. See the extract from Forbes Macgregor's poem on page 64. Excavation in the Kirk has revealed the remains of Marlin's Wynd over which the Kirk was built.

The Tron suffered a reduction in size with the building of the Bridges near to it in the 1780's, and the original wooden spire of the church was destroyed in the great conflagration of Edinburgh which broke out on the night of Monday 15th November 1824 and which destroyed most of the buildings on the south side of the High Street from the Tron to Parliament Hall. The Tron Kirk was, of course, not the only building to be affected by the erection of the North and South Bridges. The house in which Robert Fergusson was born is traditionally said to have been in Cap-and-Feather Close which was demolished in 1763 to facilitate the building of the North Bridge. Recently, however, Stuart Kay has suggested that the poet was born in Con's Close which was to the west of the Cap-and-Feather Close which was demolished and on the opposite side of the High Street between the present Covenant Close and Old Assembly Close; Con's Close was devastated by the fire of 1824 and is now covered by Tron Square. A sign on Old Assembly Close points down to Tron Square. Stuart Kay's essay on Fergusson is to be found in the first number of *New Caledonian Mercury*, September 1989. The original *Caledonian Mercury* printed Robert Burns's "Address to Edinburgh" and "Address to a Haggis" whilst he was first in Edinburgh from 28th November 1786 to 5th May 1787.

Continuing up the Royal Mile from Old Assembly Close we come to the entrance to Old Fishmarket Close where Daniel Defoe, an English spy, lived whilst the Union of Parliaments was being arranged. The public hangman also lived here. A Mercat Cross has stood near here since at least the fourteenth century. Its second site was here from 1617 until 1756 and its position is now marked by an octagonal design in the roadway. This Cross was removed but restored and returned to the High Street in 1885. The present Cross stands a few yards further up the High Street close to St Giles' Church.

Behind today's Cross are the formal Georgian buildings of Parliament Square. Behind that neo-classical frontage is Parliament Hall which survived the great fire of 1824. We go along the side of St Giles and turn right to the equestrian statue of Charles II who is

The Mercat Cross

portrayed as if an Imperial Roman Emperor even if his statue does not quite match that of Marcus Aurelius in Michelangelo's Piazza del Campidoglio in Rome. The statue of Charles was erected here in 1685, the year of that arrogant monarch's death. His brother James VII was proclaimed King of Scots on 10th February 1685. On 23rd December 1688 James fled to France and before that on 10th December a mob broke into Holyrood and at the Mercat Cross not many yards from here a bonfire was made of woodwork from the Chapel Royal. In all but law the Stewarts were off the throne of Scotland. A long day's change for them, as it was, or had been, for Edinburgh which they deserted.

We move on to Parliament Hall which does not advertise itself, but it is in the corner of the Square to the right of the statue. A nameplate says, "Parliament Hall - Court of Session". Although now sadly impoverished in the use made of it, Parliament Hall remains architecturally impressive. It was occupied by the Thrie Estates, or the Scottish Parliament, until the Union of the Scottish and English Parliaments in 1707. Quite apart from the political implications ot that Union, another fine ceremonial occasion was lost to the Scottish capital, perhaps symbolising the political implications. I refer to the Riding of the Scottish Parliament - a procession from Holyrood to Parliament Close which, in the words of Walter Scott in *Redgauntlet*, "new-fangled affection has termed a square".

James V

Parliament Hall was built between 1632 and 1640, the great oak hammerbeam roof being completed in 1639 but the fine south window is of later date. It was made in the Royal Bavarian Glass Factory in Munich and installed in 1868. It shows James V inaugurating the Court of Session and College of Justice on 27th May 1532; on the throne to the left of the King is Margaret Tudor, mother of James V and sister of Henry VIII of England. This is a relationship which led to James VI assuming the crown of England as well as that of Scotland. Today in Parliament Hall lawyers walk, or sit in the side benches, in discussion with their clients or colleagues. Here is to be seen a statue of Walter Scott.

Leaving Parliament Hall we go left and round the corner to pass the Signet Library which is private but has one of the finest rooms in Edinburgh. Ahead is the large statue of the 5th Duke of Buccleuch; Walter Scott dedicated his *Minstrelsy of the Scottish Border*, which included a version of the ballad of "Marie Hamilton", see page 44, to the 4th Duke. In front of the statue set into the cobbles in brass are the dates 1678, 1610, 1386. These relate to the building and extending of the Old Tolbooth and the many brass plates in this area indicate the outline of the building. Nearer to St Giles are other dates set in the cobbles and in front of these is a heart-shaped design. In *The Heart of Midlothian* Walter Scott wrote, "The Tolbooth of Edinburgh is called the Heart of Midlothian".

This Old Tolbooth was where Marie Hamilton of the ballad was brought for trial. In its early years sometimes Parliament met within its walls and latterly it was used solely as a prison. It was demolished in 1817. A New Tolbooth, which stood to the south-west of St Giles, was built in 1562 and demolished in 1811. It was the meeting place of the Scottish Parliament until Parliament Hall was built in 1639.

Standing on the heart shape outside St Giles we can see above the west door the great west window which is dedicated to the memory of Robert Burns. If we look again even higher we can see on the skyline, shining and moving in the sunlight, the golden

The Tolbooth

14

air-cock of St Giles. All who have read Robert Fergusson's poem, "Auld Reikie", see page 38, must hear his lines,

> Now morn, with bonny purpie-smiles,
> Kisses the air-cock o' St Giles;

Alongside these lines, on page 38, I have put other fine lines by Norman MacCaig that refer to that "golden coxcomb".

Leaving the air-cock shining in the sunlight, we enter the church by the west door, to the left of which are statues of Gavin Douglas and John Knox. I leave identification of the other figures to those who take this walk. I like to walk a few yards into the Church and then turn to see the light-filled images of the West, or Burns, window. It is the work of Leifur Breidfjord. In the upper five panels are images which celebrate the brotherhood of man expressed so powerfully by Burns in his poem "A Man's a Man for A'That". An inscription on the floor reads, "This window celebrates Robert Burns poet of humanity 1985". In the topmost part of the window there is a light-filled symbol of the supremacy of love which found expression, in a diversity of attitudes, in the songs of Burns including the unmatchable simplicity of "Ae Fond Kiss", see page 70.

Turning to look down the nave we turn right and come to a fine plaque in memory of Robert Louis Stevenson whose roots were very much in Edinburgh, although he had a tendency to remember the harsher elements of the weather of his native city, as in the extract from his poem "Ille Terrarum" printed on page 39. On the wall at right angles to this large memorial are five smaller ones. The third of them is in memory of John Stuart Blackie who was Professor of Greek in Edinburgh University and a nationally-known eccentric. His versification on Jenny Geddes is on page 50.

To move from the lyricism of the Burns window and the creative writings of Stevenson to the politics of Charles I is to move from the sublime intelligence of poets, great and minor, to the ridiculous ideas of a stubborn and power-mad monarch. When Charles came to Edinburgh in 1633 his ecclesiastical aims were similar to those of his father James VI when he came in 1617. Like his father, Charles was welcomed to Edinburgh with grand ceremony; again William Drummond wrote a work for the occasion, see page 49. Unlike his father who knew the Scots, Charles did not not back down on the ecclesiastical question. In making Edinburgh an episcopal see he transformed what had been the High Kirk of St Giles into St Giles' Cathedral. On 23rd July 1637 when the new Service Book (Laud's Liturgy), which many Scots saw as savouring of popery, was introduced to a large congregation in St Giles there was a riot in the church. The popular tradition is that Jenny Geddes threw a stool at James Hannay, Dean of the Cathedral, as he read from Laud's Liturgy, crying, "Daur ye say mass at my lug?". Tradition also has it that she continued to have a cabbage stall in the High Street long after this day of her great fame. There is a plaque to Hannay in St Giles which has the words, "He was the first and the last who read the Service Book in this Church" and today "replicas" of Jenny Geddes's stool can be bought in the Cathedral shop.

Next to the Blackie plaque in St Giles is one to the fine novelist Margaret Oliphant. Her golden head reminds me of that of Clarinda in Canongate Churchyard. To the left of this plaque is the small memorial to Robert Fergusson and standing at it we can see, on a large pillar over to the left, a plaque in memory of Gavin Douglas; it is of brass and its red and black lettering informs us, "Provost of this Collegiate Church 1501. Afterwards Bishop of Dunkeld". Although accurate, these words give a false impression of the life of

Robert Louis Stevenson

Riot in St Giles

this great poet. His machinations and taking up of arms are very much another aspect of Bishop Douglas who had aimed by the use of force to acquire the abbacy of Arbroath and the see of St Andrews. He spent some time in 1515 as a prisoner in Edinburgh castle which he described as standing on, "that wyndy and richt vnpleasant royk of Edinburgh".

Standing at the Douglas plaque we can see over to the right a white marble effigy with colours from a stained-glass window lighting the wall above it. The effigy is of James Graham, Marquis of Montrose, one of the great heroes of Scottish history. For a poem on "heroes" see that by Norman MacCaig on page 80. It was a dark May day in 1650 when Montrose swung from thirty feet of rope at Edinburgh Cross. On the eve of his brutal execution he wrote his famous poem which is printed on page 51. The final four lines are inscribed below the effigy here in St Giles although they differ from the text I print. Montrose fought first for the Covenanters against Charles and signed the National Covenant an original parchment of which, signed at Linlithgow in 1638, can be seen to the right of the effigy. Montrose changed sides to support the King and his poem written on the execution of Charles is on page 51. After the Restoration in 1660 Charles II had Montrose's remains laid to rest in St Giles. Inlaid in the decorated floor of the church within a simple border of stones are the words," Montrose 1661".

The aisle in which the Montrose effigy stands had been donated by Walter Chepman in 1513 and dedicated in memory of James IV and his Queen. Facing the Montrose effigy is a plaque, of 1879, to Chepman who with Androw Myllar introduced printing into Scotland. They were given a patent by James IV dated 15th September 1507. There has been some debate about the site of the first Scottish printing-house but it was probably at the Cowgate end of Blackfriars Wynd. Standing in the aisle donated by Walter Chepman and dedicated in memory of James IV and his Queen in 1513 and facing the words of Montrose, we are in the world of a soldier-courtier-scholar poet set alongside that of the civilising influence of a printer of poems by William Dunbar and Robert Henryson in the reign of James IV, a renaissance prince. It can be said that with the few poems of Montrose we come to the end of the Scottish courtly tradition in verse.

James I's "proper hand"

James VI, at the age of 14

Grassmarket Edinburgh

W Geikie

17

WALK 2
FROM WORLD'S END CLOSE
TO BEDLAM

Robert Fergusson

We begin this Walk 2 at World's End Close which is, as Gordon Wright says in his *A Guide to the Royal Mile*, "The last close at the bottom of the High Street before the city wall and the outside world". Or as Robert Garioch wrote in his poem, 'To Robert Fergusson',

> To World's End Close frae Ramsay Lane
> we'd ding Auld Reekie's back rigg-bane.
> Whan Ne'er-gate's ten-hour bell had gane
> that wadnae daunt us;

Psychologically this has been an important place in the minds of the citizens of Edinburgh. We pass the entrance to Tweeddale Court, in which the Scottish Poetry Library is situated, and continue past Blackfriars Street to South Bridge with the Tron Kirk opposite. We turn down South Bridge, our destination being Chambers Street which we turn into and after some 20 yards see on the right Guthrie Street where there is a tablet with these words, 'Near this spot stood the house in which Sir Walter Scott was born 15th August 1771'. Scott himself wrote, "I was born, as I believe, on the 15th August 1771, in a house belonging to my father, at the head of College Wynd. It was pulled down with others to make room for the northern front of the new college". In 1771 College Wynd rose from the Cowgate to where we now stand. The name survives in a few yards of street in Cowgate. Here in Chambers Street opposite the Scott tablet runs the northern wall of what is now named Old College.

Robert Garioch

We retrace our steps along Chambers Street with the excellently proportioned windows of Old College on our right. We cross South Bridge and turn right past Infirmary Street to stand in front of Thin's bookshop facing the imposing front of Old College opposite. Above the perfectly proportioned arches is an inscription in formal Roman capitals. The first line is, ACADEMIA JACOBI VI SCOTORVM REGIS and the seventh and final is ARCHITECTO ROBERTO ADAM a name which explains the reason for the perfect proportions of Old College. Looking higher, there, shining in the sunlight against the moving clouds, is another fine golden climax to an Edinburgh building. It is a nude male figure holding high the flaming torch of knowledge; a superb image and not by Adam or Playfair but added, as was the dome on which it stands, in 1884.

We cross South Bridge, traffic permitting, to go through the arch of Old College, and then into the quadrangle. My preference is to walk straight across this beautiful space, ignoring the parked cars, under the eye of the formal clock with its gold roman numerals, to climb the formal steps beneath it. Standing on these steps we have another dramatic sighting of that "golden boy".

Walter Scott

Here was the old collegiate church of St Mary-in-the-Fields or, as it was termed in popular usage, Kirk o' Field. It was so named because it stood in open fields beyond the King's Wall of 1450, although it was within the later Flodden Wall. Today the quadrangle of Old College occupies the site of the church. It was at Kirk o' Field that

Hugh MacDiarmid

Mrs Alison Cockburn

Darnley, husband of Mary Queen of Scots, was murdered early on the morning of 10th February 1567. Darnley is yet another poet and his poem addressed to Queen Mary is printed on page 42.

Our next destination is the Talbot Rice Gallery to the right. Immediately inside the Gallery is a maquette of the Hugh MacDiarmid Memorial which stands above Langholm, Dumfriesshire, birthplace of the poet in 1892. The memorial is by Jake Harvey and the maquette is dated '82. Although not in any true sense an Edinburgh poet, Hugh MacDiarmid visited the city frequently in the years when he lived near Biggar, from 1952 until his death in 1978. MacDiarmid's greatest long poem is *A Drunk Man Looks at the Thistle*, 1926, which was written whilst he was living in Montrose. See my reference to the publication of this masterpiece in my poem on page 81.

We leave the Talbot Rice Gallery by a door to the right of the maquette, that takes us into West College Street where we turn left. Facing us at its end is a pedestrian subway or underpass bearing the sign Potterrow Port. Again we are at the Flodden Wall. Although strictly not part of an Old Town walk, we now make a detour. Old Town purists should continue along Lothian Street to Lauriston Place. Following a lane to the left of the subway we walk along Potterrow to what is now a large car park. This is where Mrs McLehose, or Robert Burns's Clarinda, had her flat in General's Entry, Potterrow. After some controversy that led to questions being asked in the House of Commons, a plaque was put on a wall of Bristo Street Technical Institute in 1937. It read "Near this spot resided 'Clarinda' friend of Robert Burns". I hope that it has survived.

We continue down Chapel Street to West Nicolson Street where, at no. 18, the poetry magazine *Lines Review* was published and printed between 1957 and 1960, although no. 13 of the magazine gives two addresses, one being 18 W. Nicolson Street and the other 33 Marchmont Road where early numbers of this pioneering and long-lived poetry magazine were printed and published by Callum Macdonald, who still publishes it.

We cross to the other side of Chapel Street to where an old stone wall begins and a plaque informs that Mrs Cockburn, author of a version of the lamenting song "The Flowers of the Forest", "lies buried near here". She is buried in the kirkyard enclosed by the wall. Mrs Cockburn saw Burns when he was in Edinburgh in 1786 and wrote an interesting letter on how he behaved, see Walk 3.

Going on from the grave of Mrs Cockburn we come to Buccleuch Street where Burns had digs with Willie Nicol (1744-97) during three of his visits to Edinburgh. The actual building may have been above Buccleuch Pend which gave access to St Patrick Square. In a letter to Archibald Lawrie of 14th August 1787, Burns says "Here I sit, in the attic storey, alias, the garret". In a letter to Robert Ainslie of 23rd August he writes, "Mr Nicol on the opposite side of the table . . . gabbling Latin so loud that I cannot hear what my own soul is saying in my own scull". This gabbler was a classics master in the High School and on 25th August Burns left with Nicol on his tour of the Highlands. Nicol is the Willie of the song "Willie Brew'd a Peck o' Maut", see page 66 and see Burns's epitaph for him on page 76.

Burns returned to Buccleuch Street on 16th September 1787 and spent another ten days or so there in March 1788. During his visit to Edinburgh from 20th October 1787 to 18th February 1788 he had lodgings with another High School teacher, William

Cruickshank. His flat was outside the Old Town in St James's Square where today we have the St James Centre, a shopping precinct. It was from no. 2 (afterwards no. 30) St James's Square that Burns first corresponded with Mrs McLehose, or Clarinda, who said she walked below his window overlooking St James's Square in the hope of seeing him. Burns, who was again in an attic although he had two rooms, wrote to Clarinda," I am certain I saw you, Clarinda; but you didn't look to a proper storey for a poet's lodging". And the lady replied, being perhaps as full of imaginary walks as any letter-writing poet, "All the time my eye soared to poetic heights, *alias garrets, but not a glimpse of you could I obtain*".

Clarinda's House

Returning from this flight into the world of verbalising lovers to today's Buccleuch Street, we go along the righthand side of Buccleuch Place to steps which lead up to the David Hume Tower in George Square. We turn left past the Adam Ferguson building and George Square Theatre to the University Library in which is to be seen a portrait of Hugh MacDiarmid and also a large archive of his papers. Continuing round to the West side of this George Square we pass the School of Scottish Studies at no. 27, which has a large treasure-house of recordings of folksongs and story, to come to no. 25 which was the home of Walter Scott 1774-97, his family having moved from College Wynd soon after he was born. We continue to the top of the terrace where we leave the Square by the road to the left of it and continue up Middle Meadow Walk to cross to Lauriston Place. We have rejoined the purists who did not detour out of the Old Town. We go along Lauriston Place past a surviving part of the Telfer Wall and at the end of its few yards, to the grounds of George Heriot's School. In the quad stands a statue of George Heriot who features in Fergusson's poem "The Ghaists: A Kirk-yard Eclogue", see page 74. Looking over to the right from the school's driveway we can see yet another dramatic Edinburgh skyline with the beautiful crown steeple of Saint Giles' Church balanced by the contrasting lower-key mass of Greyfriars Kirk. We continue along Lauriston Place to turn into Heriot Place. Here is another section of the massive Telfer Wall and filling the skyline is the Castle. The wall becomes castellated some yards before Heriot Place runs into the Vennel and facing us is the Flodden Wall and also a unique survivor—one of the towers of the 1513 wall. The Castle is even more massive on the skyline. We go down steps, past Brown's Place, to the Grassmarket.

The Vennel

To stand in today's Grassmarket with the castle three hundred feet above is to be in a space that is not so very different from what must have been here in medieval times although the buildings were different. We are at the site of the West Port, or gate, of the Flodden Wall. This West Port was ceremonially a lesser gate than the Netherbow but it was through it that travellers from the south-west, west and north-west came, including Robert Burns from Ayrshire in 1786 (Walk 3), and Charles 1 in 1633 (Walk 1).

Moving from the site of the old gate to a few yards east of the Vennel we come to Porteous' Pend. It is named after the infamous John Porteous who, as a commander of the City Guard, ordered innocent people to be fired upon and slaughtered here in the Grassmarket; the result was the riots of 1736 which bear his name. A crowd gathered after dark on 7th September at the western suburb of Portsburgh, marched on the West Port which they took over, as they did the Cowgate and Netherbow ports, overpowered the soldiers of the City Guard, seizing their muskets and Lochaber axes. Some 4000 strong, they then marched on the Tolbooth prison on the

High Street (see Walk 1), burned down the door and dragged Porteous out and down to the Grassmarket where they hanged him from a dyer's pole. No damage to property was done, nor looting, and tradition has it that they even left a guinea for the shopkeeper from whose shop in the West Bow they took the rope for the hanging; the shop today is Ye Olde Curiosity Shoppe at West Bow/Victoria Street which we will see when we reach the east end of the Grassmarket. Tradition also has it that some very eminent citizens, dressed as women, took part in this riot. The classic unrivallable description of that dark night is by Walter Scott in *The Heart of Midlothian*.

Leaving Porteous' Pend to its echoes we cross the street diagonally to the White Hart Inn. Writing from Dumfries to Mrs McLehose on 23rd November 1791 Robert Burns wrote, "I shall be in Edinburgh on Tuesday first . . . at Mr Mackay's White Hart Inn, Grassmarket, where I shall put up". He seems to have been there from 29th November to 6th December and, as a plaque outside the Inn states, it was his last visit to Edinburgh. A notice outside the Inn informs us that in 1803 William Wordsworth and his sister Dorothy also put up at this inn.

We continue along the street past the foot of Castle Wynd South to The Last Drop pub, so named because of the public hangings in this market area. Over in the centre of the street is a walled memorial garden within which we can read the words, "On this spot many martyrs and covenanters died for the protestant faith". A plaque, unveiled in 1988, commemorates the 350th anniversary of the first signing of the National Covenant, which took place in Greyfriars Kirk on 28th February 1638; the plaque lists some convenanters executed here in the Grassmarket, at the Mercat Cross in the High Street and at Gallowlee, Leith Walk.

To the left of the little garden is West Bow and facing us is the famous experimental theatre, the Traverse, and to the left the old West Bow Well. We go up West Bow to see Ye Olde Curiosity Shoppe from where the rope that hanged Porteous was stolen. Here West Bow becomes Victoria Street which was built in the late 1830s and it, and Victoria Terrace at a higher level, divided West Bow which previously ran right up to the Royal Mile. The upper end of West Bow was called the Head of the Bow, now Upper Bow which can be reached by steps in Victoria Street opposite Preservation Hall. In Upper Bow stood the infamous house of Major Thomas Weir, who is mentioned in Robert Fergusson's poem "The Ghaists: A Kirk-yard Eclogue", see page 74. Major Weir, who lived a respectable and seemingly God-fearing life in his house in the Head of the Bow with his sister, became ill and confessed to acts of incest, bestiality, sorcery and murder. He was strangled and burnt at the stake near today's Picardy Place on 12th April 1670; his sister, however, was hanged in the Grassmarket. For a century their empty house in West Bow was a place to avoid, not least by the young James Boswell who went to school in the West Bow.

We return to the east end of the Grassmarket where we turn left into the few yards of Cowgatehead to stand at the entrance to Cowgate. On the skyline can be seen another golden weather-cock, that of the Magdalen Chapel which was built in the 1540s. This is a building of major architectural and historical importance; it is now owned by the Scottish Reformation Society whose premises are almost overhead on George IV Bridge, the rather gloomy arch of which crosses the Cowgate a few yards along from Magdalen Chapel. Our route, however, is up Candlemaker Row following the wall of Greyfriars Kirkyard. At the top of the Row stands the famous

White Hart Inn

Greyfriars Kirk

statue of Greyfriars Bobby, see my poem on page 75. We turn into Greyfriars Kirkyard where a stone commemorating Bobby faces us. To the left is a notice board listing the names of famous men buried here. The monument on the wall of a house to the left is that of the famous Mylne family whose work as masons are encountered in these walks.

George Heriot's School

We take the path to the right, past a notice board giving directions to the grave of Bobby's master. The large monuments set against the back of the houses of Candlemaker Row include some of the oldest in the churchyard. Our destination is one near the end of those. It bears an hour-glass and skull and crossbones which have been eroded by time. The initials on the memorial are GH and the date 1610 can just be read, after the worn Latin inscription, at the lower right-hand corner. This is the memorial of George Heriot. His son succeeded him in the family jewellery business in a stall near to St. Giles' Church and was appointed goldsmith to James VI. George Heriot junior became a very rich man, leaving his fortune for the upbringing and education of fatherless boys and the founding of "Heriot's Hospital", today's George Heriot's School which we can see through the trees to the right of the church. The building of the "Hospital" began in 1628 but, for a diversity of reasons, it was not till 1659 that thirty fatherless boys were admitted. In his poem "The Ghaists: A Kirk-yard Eclogue", see page 74, Robert Fergusson has Heriot speak as one of his two ghosts. The other is George Watson, an accountant to the Bank of Scotland, who endowed what is today George Watson's School, and whose grave is in this kirkyard. With typical Edinburgh, or Scottish, irreverence, Heriot was nicknamed "Jinglin Geordie", although it has been suggested that it was James VI who so named him. He has the honour of a pub of that name in Fleshmarket Close which is on the route of Walk 3. The pub sign is as witty as his nickname. As Robert Fergusson indicates in his poem, the statue of him in George Heriot's School was busked, or dressed, with flowers by the boys each year, on the first Monday of June. Heriot is buried in London in St Martin's-in-the-Fields.

George Heriot

In his poem Robert Fergusson refers to "Adam's tomb" which is that of William Adam the architect, father of the architects Robert and James, but to indicate the position of the graves of all the famous men in this kirkyard is beyond the scope of this walk. Here is buried the humanist George Buchanan who died in 1582 and there is a stained glass window in his memory within Greyfriars Kirk. Also buried here are William Creech—Burns's publisher—Captain Porteous and the great Gaelic poet Duncan Ban Macintyre who was, almost unbelievably in its inappropriateness, a member of the City Guard. He died in 1812. The other major poet buried here is Allan Ramsay. The place of his burial is not known but there has been conjecture as to where it is. In his book *Silences That Speak*, William Pitcairn Anderson quotes from the burial entry, "1758 Jany. 9. Mr Allan Ramsay, Lyes 5 dble. paces S.W. the blew stone. A poet. Old age.". The site of the blew stone is not known. We leave Heriot's memorial to walk round to the far side of the church. Go into the church to see the Buchanan window. Leaving the church we go round to its south wall where there is a tablet to the memory of Allan Ramsay which was placed there sixty-two years after the poet's death.

George Buchanan

Leaving Greyfriars Kirkyard into Greyfriars Place we look to the right and across to a converted church, now the Bedlam Theatre. The theatre is on the site of an earlier building that is important to the history of Scottish poetry. Here, as the name of the

Captain of the City Guard

theatre indicates, was the Edinburgh Bedlam which was an annexe to Darien House, the old Workhouse which stood in the triangle formed today by Forrest Road, Teviot Place and Bristo Place, see Robert Garioch's poem on page 54. The Telfer wall ran round the Bedlam and the Flodden Wall also passed near where we stand. These city walls were intended to keep invaders out. The Bedlam walls were, of course, intended to keep people in to lie in squalor on a bed of loose uncovered straw and beseiged by the wailings of their fellow inmates.

It was to the Edinburgh Bedlam that, in June 1774, the poet Robert Fergusson was taken, raving, as a pauper lunatic. It was known, grimly, as the Schelles (Cells). There on 17th October 1774 Fergusson died, aged twenty-four years and one month. The entry in the minute book of the Charity Workhouse reads "Mr Ferguson, in the Cels".

Robert Fergusson

23

Tradition points in the above engraving to the first window on the right of the Close of Lady Stair's Close as that of the room in which Burns first lodged in Edinburgh.

Top: Anchor Close, Warriston Close and Advocate's Close and John Dowie landlord of a tavern in Libberton Wynd frequented by Robert Burns.

Lower: Lady Stair's Close and John Dowie's Tavern renamed Burns Tavern.

WALK 3
FROM WORLD'S END CLOSE TO CASTLE ROCK

High School Building of 1578

Second High School

We begin as with Walk 2 at World's End Close and walk the few yards to Tweeddale Court which we enter, going through the fine wrought-iron gate to the Scottish Poetry Library, see poems on page 78. We leave the Library, passing the old premises of Oliver & Boyd, see the poem on page 78, turning right to go through New Skinner's Close into Blackfriars Street, previously named Blackfriars Wynd which is the title of Donald Campbell's play from which his song on page 60 is taken. Today this street is gradually going upmarket but it was most certainly not a salubrious street in the last quarter of the nineteenth century, which may be the period of Donald Campbell's play.

We go down to Cowgate and facing us is High School Wynd. For a short time in 1554 the High School was in a building in Blackfriars Wynd that had once been the residence of Cardinal Beaton. That house has gone but an inscription on the building at the corner here marks the site. We walk up High School Wynd to High School Yards. Here was the High School building that was erected in 1578 and stood within an open space that was known, as today, as the High School Yards. This building with its frontage facing north ran east and west. It was the building that Robert Fergusson entered on his first day as a pupil at the High School in 1758. It is perhaps an example of serendipity that I know that this was the year of Allan Ramsay's death, but it does seem to have some symbolic significance.

Going past High School Yards we come on the left to gates that face Infirmary Street. Through these gates is the High School building which replaced that in which Fergusson sat as a pupil. The building we face was that entered by Walter Scott when he became a pupil of the School in 1779 soon after the new building opened. In 1829 the High School moved from here to Calton Hill and it was to that building that Robert Garioch and Norman MacCaig went. In his poem "To Robert Fergusson", see page 54, Garioch recognises that he and Fergusson had a kinship in attending the High School.

Robert Garioch, like Norman MacCaig and Walter Scott, was a graduate of Edinburgh University and standing in front of the old High School building we see, glowing against the pure blue sky in the northern sunlight of Edinburgh, the "golden boy" of the University's Old College. That the sun shines each time I make these walks is no creative licence but it may be that I wait for a fine day before going on a walkabout.

We turn right to go back down to Cowgate. In the nineteenth century this was a very poor and isolated quarter of the city with a large Irish population. James Connolly, who was a member of the Provisional Government of the Irish Republic, was born at no. 107 Cowgate on 5th June 1868; he was executed on 12th May 1916 at Kilmainham Jail, Dublin. The Cowgate remained a street that was avoided by outsiders when I first ventured into it in the mid fifties. For a slightly later view of how the Cowgate was regarded see Donald Campbell's poem on page 59. In earlier times it was quite different, being "ubnihil humile aut rusticum, sed omnia magnifica". In 1550 Alexander Alesius wrote, to use a translation from his Latin by Hume Brown which I take from David Daiches' *Edinburgh*, "From King's Street to north and south extend numberless lesser streets, all adorned with imposing buildings, such, for example, as the Cowgate (Via Vaccarum) where the nobility and the chief men of the city reside, and in which are the palaces of the officers of state, and where is nothing mean or tasteless but all is magnificent."

We cross this Cowgate to turn left to St Cecilia's Hall, built by Robert Mylne in 1763 for the Musical Society of Edinburgh and based on the Opera House at Parma. The beautiful interior has been excellently restored by Edinburgh University. We pass Niddry Street where Robert Fergusson went to school. Here also is Bannerman's pub which is near to where was Luckie Middlemass's famous oyster tavern which is mentioned in Fergussons's poem "Caller Oysters", see page 64.

Reaching the foot of Blair street opposite the arches of 369 Gallery we continue a few yards along to see today's College Wynd which once went up to where today stands Edinburgh University's Old College and at the top of which was the birthplace of Walter Scott. We return to Blair Street and go up its left-hand side with the Tron Kirk looking down on us. On reaching the High Street and the Kirk we pause before turning up the High Street to pause again by Covenant Close and Old Assembly Close, to think of the birthplace of Robert Fergusson perhaps being near here, see Walk 1.

Robert Burns
Reversed portrait,
after Beugo,
by Halpen,
in the Dublin
pirated edition.

We cross the street to Anchor Close where a plaque at its entrance informs that here was the printing house of William Smellie who printed the Edinburgh edition of Burns's poems. Tradition has it that Burns corrected the proofs of his book sitting on a stool in the printing-house. The stool he is said to have sat on is now in Lady Stair's House Museum which is further up the Royal Mile, see Douglas Fraser's poem on page 77. Smellie was undoubtably a character, described by Burns as, "Veteran in Genius, Wit, and B—dry". He was the founder of the Crochallan Fencibles who met in Dawnay Douglas's Anchor Tavern which stood here in Anchor Close. By introducing Burns to this somewhat disreputable club, Smellie enabled the poet to learn and write bawdy verses. In a letter to Peter Hill, dated February 1794, Burns asked, "How is old sinful Smellie coming on with this world?" For Burns's friendly character sketch of Smellie see page 77.

William Smellie

We go down today's narrow Anchor Close to pass a doorway with sombre words of advice, "Lord be Merciful to Me", to reach Cockburn Street and looking uphill to the right can see over the street the entrance to the section of Fleshmarket Close that leads to Market Street. In that Close is the Jinglin' Geordie pub with a sign that is a witty portrait of George Heriot who features in both the previous walks, and in Fergusson's poem on page 74.

A little way down the left-hand side of Cockburn Street from Anchor Close is a blocked entrance on which a plaque informs that here is, or was, Craig's Close "site of Cape Club, spiritual home of Robert Fergusson". In Fergusson's day one of the characteristics of the town was the tavern clubs in which kindred spirits met in the evenings for good conversation, the singing of songs and the drinking of good ale, whisky or claret. The Cape Club was one of these and often met in James Mann's in Craig's Close. The poet joined the Club on 10th October 1772 assuming, as was the way with such clubs with their mock ceremonials, the name Sir Precenter, see Sydney Goodsir Smith's poem on page 63 and also Fergusson's lines on page 65. The Cape had a mixed membership, biased towards literary, artistic, theatrical and antiquarian personages, although the infamous Deacon William Brodie, used by Robert Louis Stevenson as a model for his Dr Jekyll and Mr Hyde, was a member; later Henry Raeburn the painter was a member. The Club met every evening including Sundays about seven o'clock and members left about eleven or perhaps just before ten - not at

Deacon Brodie

ten as this was the hour when "the noisy ten-hour drum" of the City Guard, "the black banditti" of Fergusson's poem on page 55, announced that it was time for pouring of rubbish from the houses - this known as "Gardyloo!". As Alexander Hutchison writes in his poem "Annals of Enlightenment", see page 82, "At ten, a drum/for clart and creesh/on close and vennel".

Moving down Cockburn Street from the site of Craig's Close we come to Warriston's Close, where Robert Fergusson latterly lived. Half way up its leg-wearying steps we pause for breath at a plaque which indicates the site of a house that John Knox lived in from 1560 to 1566. On reaching the High Street above the entrance to that steep Close lettering informs, "Writers' Court leading to Warriston's Close". In Writers' Court lived Alexander Nasmyth who painted Burns's portrait. It should perhaps be pointed out that the "Writers" were lawyers and not literary men.

Turning up the High Street we come to Advocate's Close where a plaque informs of the famous men who lived there. One was, the plaque informs, "Andrew Crosbie, the jovial Councillor Pleydell". This assumes a certain knowledge of the novels of Walter Scott as we are not told who this jovial gentleman was; in fact he appears in *Guy Mannering*. This is a far more interesting Close than Warriston's; a few yards down it are inscriptions on two lintels dated 1590. Beyond these are the offices of the Old Town Trust and yet further down is a doorway with the words, "He that tholes overcomes". My inclination is to stop here and turn back up to the High Street, but the way to explore these Closes is to go up and down them as the mood takes one

Returning to the High Street we cross to St Giles and to its east end by the Mercat Cross. Here in front of St Giles stood the Luckenbooths which were locked shops as opposed to open stalls. In the eighteenth century this was the busy centre of the old city's life. The Luckenbooths stood close to and parallel with the north wall of St Giles. In Dunbar's time the projecting "foirstairis" darkened the interior of the houses, as he complained, as he did of the squalor of the "stynkand style" that ran through the Luckenbooths, see page 72.

This was bad enough but in later times the Luckenbooths also created a congested High Street at this point, although a pedestrian area would have solved that problem. In the narrow passageway between the shops and the wall of the church there were from the sixteenth century between the buttresses of the church crowded rows of tiny open stalls known as the krames, many of which sold toys; to Lord Cockburn in the nineteenth century these were, "the paradise of childhood". Round the corner of St Giles, into what is today Parliament Square, were other little shops some of which were the premises of watchmakers and jewellers. One of these jewellers was George Heriot who was goldsmith to King James VI from 1601, see Walk 2 and Robert Fergusson's poem on page 74 in which Heriot is one of the ghosts.

Allan Ramsay as an entrepreneur for Scottish culture is a giant in the history of Scottish poetry. So it was an important day for poetry when in 1726 he opened a new bookshop at the east end of the Luckenbooths. His first bookshop, which he opened when he gave up his trade of wig-maker, was opposite Niddry Wynd, now Street. It has been said that Ramsay's shop in the Luckenbooths became the "Hub of the Universe" and certainly all manner of men foregathered there.

A successor to Ramsay as a bookseller in the building at the east end of the Luckenbooths was William Creech. With his shop in the five-storied building he was continuing a tradition and not least the practice of establishing a meeting-place for

Andrew Crosbie "Pleydell"

Creech's shop

Libberton wynd from the Cowgate

Lawn market from above the West Bow

The illustrations on this and the facing page are reproduced from very fine etchings by Walter Geikie. Other etchings by Geikie are reproduced on pages 17, 33, 51, 52, 58, 61 and the family group on page 67. Geikie was born in Charles Street on 9th November 1795 and died in another house in the same street in 1837. Before he was two years old Geikie was struck by what has been described as a nervous fever which left him deaf and dumb. Although in no way as popular as John Kay versions of whose etchings also appear in this book, Geikie reveals other aspects of the Old Town of Edinburgh.

The drawings by Kay are those of John Dowie , Deacon Brodie, Captains of the City Guard, The Knowing One, Courtship, the small figures on page 63 , Duke and Duchess and Lord Monboddo on page 71 and Two Shadows in Conversation.

those interested in literature. In the mornings Creech entertained the *literati* and printers in his house in Craig's Close opposite his shop. A small plaque to the right of the main entrance to the City Chambers building marks the entrance to this Close, the closed other end of which we saw in Cockburn Street. In the afternoon Creech crossed the road to his shop in the Luckenbooths where the flow of company continued until four when he went home for the day. Of course this socialising was good for business and this small man-about-town certainly had a head for business.

When Robert Burns came to Edinburgh in 1778 he came to Creech's shop to negotiate terms for the publication of a new edition of his poems. So as I stand by the side of St Giles I can see Burns here outside Creech's shop looking down the long telescope of the Royal Mile to that ever-surprising glimpse of the Forth at its far end. In the end Creech cheated the poet out of his copyright and took no risks with the first printing of what is now termed the Edinburgh edition of Burns's poems, liability being with the poet to pay bills if sales did not cover these. In their early dealings, however, there seems to have been little acrimony and Creech, who was an esteemed publisher, did publish the edition Burns had come to Edinburgh for. So it is appropriate that Burns immortalised Creech in his poem "To William Creech", see page 76, and also in the character sketch of him that I print on page 77. Creech died in 1815 and, like Allan Ramsay, is buried in Greyfriars Kirkyard. The Luckenbooths were demolished two years after Creech's death.

Leaving the ghosts of the Luckenbooths we continue up the High Street past the site of the old Tolbooth or Heart of Midlothian, to cross George IV Bridge and enter the Lawnmarket section of the Royal Mile. Near here on the left-hand side, before the building of George IV Bridge destroyed it, was Libberton's Wynd, rich in the varied life styles of the Old Town that included the crude and squalid but in total is uniquely of the Old Town of Edinburgh. It was the last site for public executions and the infamous body-stealer and murderer William Burke was executed here. But here also was John Dowie's Tavern which contained several rooms including a very small one, "The Coffin" - maximum six customers - which was a favourite haunt of Robert Burns when he was in lodgings nearby. When Dowie died in 1817 the new owner put up a sign, "Burns Tavern, late John Dowie". A little further up the Lawnmarket on this side of the street is Riddle's Close and Court in which is the fine house of Bailie MacMorran where James VI attended a banquet. Later David Hume lived here before moving to another flat opposite.

Facing us across the street as we come out of Riddle's Close is James's Court but we cross the street to the entrance to Lady Stair's Close. To the right of the Close is the shop of John Morrison, Kiltmaker, and above the shop door is a notice that reads, "The house where Robert Burns lodged when in Edinburgh." The actual house has gone but this was the site of it. Robert Burns came through the West Port at the west end of the Grassmarket on Tuesday 28th November 1786, in the late afternoon. He travelled on what he called a pownie and came through the Grassmarket and up the West Bow to the Lawnmarket, in the Royal Mile, to Baxter's Close. There he shared a room, and a bed, with his friend John Richmond in the flat of Mrs Carfrae. Baxter's Close was where we now stand. From the window of Richmond's room the poet would have looked out on Lady Stair's House which still stands. He lodged here until 5th May 1787 and conquered Edinburgh.

P O E M S,

CHIEFLY IN THE

SCOTTISH DIALECT.

BY

ROBERT BURNS.

EDINBURGH.
PRINTED FOR THE AUTHOR,
AND SOLD BY WILLIAM CREECH.

M,DCC,LXXXVII.

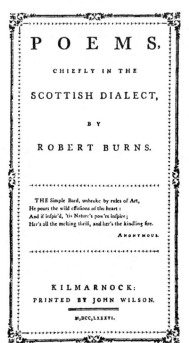

Engravings on Wood by Bewick
from designs by Thurston
Vol. 1.

Burns came to Edinburgh to follow up the success of his first book of poems - the Kilmarnock edition - by having another edition of his poems printed in the capital. He was a man come to a city that was only too ready to welcome him as a celebrity of unusual qualities. The lionising was all that any poet could ask for and it could be said that the months during which Robert Burns walked the streets of the Old Town of Edinburgh were also those when it was host to the greatest Scottish poet ever to do so. How Edinburgh received Robert Burns can be seen in a letter from Mrs Alison Cockburn to a friend. Mrs Cockburn, whose grave we detoured to in Walk 2, is now remembered for her version of the lamenting song of Flodden, "The Flowers of the Forest". In her letter she wrote, "The town is at present agog with the ploughman poet, who receives adulation with native dignity, and is the very figure of his profession, strong and coarse, but has a most enthusiastic heart of love. He has seen Duchess Gordon and all the gay world. His favourite for looks and manners is Bess Burnet - no bad judge indeed!. The man will be spoiled if he can spoil; but he keeps his simple manners, and is quite sober. No doubt he will be at the Hunters' Ball tomorrow, which has made all women and milliners mad". Bess Burnet, the daughter of Lord Monboddo, we "encountered" in Walk 1 as immortalised by Burns in a line of his poem "Address to Edinburgh", "Fair Burnet strikes th' adorin' eye".

Franklyn Bliss Snyder in his *The Life of Robert Burns* suggests that women "played a small part in Burns's life during his first winter in Edinburgh", although he thinks Margaret Chalmers may have been personally important to Burns while the Duchess of Gordon was important in giving him social acceptance. But during his second winter in Edinburgh, although polite society had lost interest in him, Mrs Agnes McLehose most certainly had not. She first spoke to Burns on 4th December 1787 and soon he was visiting her in her flat in General's Entry, Potterrow, see Walk 2. To her friends Mrs McLehose was Nancy Craig but she is immortalised as Clarinda of the famous love letters in which, responding to her suggestion, Burns was the Arcadian Sylvander. The depth of this relationship, with regard to any of the many aspects of their love, cannot be finally judged from their letters nor from the poems Burns sent to Mrs McLehose. One of these is one of his greatest songs, "Ae Fond Kiss", see page 70. He sent the poem to her on 21st December 1791 soon after he saw her for the last time.

Going through Lady Stair's Close we come to Lady Stair's House which is now a museum devoted to Robert Burns, Walter Scott and Robert Louis Stevenson. In the museum there is a copy of a painting, of 1887, by C. M. Hardie of Burns reading his poems in the Duchess of Gordon's house. Amongst those portrayed as being present were Creech, Alexander Nasmyth the painter and both Margaret Chalmers and fair Miss Burnet although Hardie does not do justice to the latter's beauty. Another in the painting is Professor Ferguson at whose house in Sciennes were held literary gatherings to which not only the established men of letters were invited but also young men of promise; so it was that Robert Burns and Walter Scott met in Ferguson's house and this is celebrated in another painting by C. M. Hardie entitled, "The Meeting of Burns and Scott". A copy of this painting is in the Castle Arms pub at the Lawnmarket end of Johnston Terrace. Professor Ferguson's house is now much changed but it is indicated by a plaque in Sciennes House Place. Also in Lady Stair's House is a painting by William Borthwick Johnstone, 1856, of Burns in James Sibbald's Circulating Library in Parliament Square. In the lower righthand corner of it is Walter Scott as a boy and Miss Burnet is a central figure. All of this is romantic nonsense but reveals the interest in both Burns and Scott in nineteenth-century Scotland. Here in the museum is also a reproduction of a painting showing Burns, and many of the famous men of Edinburgh, in the Kilwinning Masonic Lodge of Canongate in St John's Street, see Walk 1.

While Burns was in Edinburgh he arranged for a headstone to be put on Robert Fergusson's pauper's grave in Canongate Kirkyard, see Walk 1. The invoice for the stone can be seen in Lady Stair's House as can a lock of Fergusson's hair. The architect who had the headstone erected for Burns was Robert Burn and the poet paid him through Peter Hill, who was Creech's assistant during Burns's first visit to Edinburgh and acted as unofficial Edinburgh banker for the poet. Burns wrote to Hill on 5th February 1792, "I send you by the bearer, Mr Clarke, a particular friend of mine, six pounds & a shilling, which you will dispose of as follows; - £5 - 10, per acct I owe to Mr Robt. Burn, Architect, for erecting the stone over poor Ferguson. - He was two years in erecting it, after I commissioned him for it; & I have been two years paying him, after he sent me his account; so he & I are quits. - He had the hardiesse to ask me interest on the sum; but considering that the money was due by one Poet, for putting a tombstone over another, he may, with grateful surprise, thank Heaven that ever he saw a farthing of it". As an architect Burn is better known for the Nelson Monument on Calton Hill and his son, William, was responsible for putting the present grey walls around St Giles' Church.

Unlike Burns, and also Allan Ramsay, Robert Fergusson is essentially a poet of superb description and so his Edinburgh is as alive today as when he walked the streets of the eighteenth-century Old Town in the all-too-short months when he wrote his poetry. His first poem in Scots, "The Daft-Days", see page 55, was printed in *The Weekly Magazine* on 2nd January 1772. This was a dramatic printing for some readers, one of whom was to ask, "Is Allan risen frae the deid?" Allan Ramsay had died fifteen years before and in that time no-one had emerged to match his achievement in Scots.

Only two years after the publication of that first poem in Scots, the *Caledonian Mercury* noted, in February 1774, that Robert Fergusson "had a very dangerous sickness". The life-loving man of the Cape Club and the Edinburgh taverns had been seized by religious melancholy. As I described in Walk 2 he was removed, raving, as a pauper lunatic to the Edinburgh Bedlam and died on 17th October 1774 aged twenty-four years and one month.

Leaving Lady Stair's House, to the left and eastwards is Blackie House, named after John Stuart Blackie whose poem on Jenny Geddes is on page 50. It is possible to walk from Lady Stair's House to other courts without going back to the Lawnmarket but I prefer to enter each of them from the Royal Mile. The site of Boyd's Inn where Samuel Johnson first called at when he visited Edinburgh, was seen in Walk 2. From there he came to James Boswell's rooms in James's Court which we now enter by its East Entry past the Jolly Judge pub where hangs another copy of the Hardie painting of Burns reading at the Duchess of Gordon's. I refer to the Jolly Judge in my poem on page 81. In the time of Boswell and Johnson James's Court was eight stories high and had been built in the 1720's by James Brownhill whose forename lives on. David Hume also lived for a time in James's Court and the contrast between Boswell and Hume is one aspect of Alexander Hutchison's poem on page 82. Leaving the ghost of Boswell to its heaven or hell, we leave James's Court by its Mid Entry which has an informative

Head of the West Bow.

33

plaque. If theatre buffs leave by West Entry they will see an old board with the words, Traverse Theatre; today the theatre is down in the West Bow, see Walk 2.

Continuing a few yards uphill we come to the entrance to Mylne's Court in which now are Halls of Residence of Edinburgh University which were masterly works of restoration. Mylne's Court was built by one of the dynasty of master masons whom we have encountered in all of these walks. Since Boswell and Hume's time James's and Mylne's Courts have been much rebuilt but there does seem to be something unchanging about this part of the Royal Mile and here today surely Robert Fergusson and Allan Ramsay would still feel that it was their Edinburgh. For my reaction to these courts see my poem on page 75. I first knew these closes, courts, wynds and lands (tenements) off the Lawnmarket in the fifties. Then they were mostly run-down but for me they were alive with history. Today many of them have been modernised but to look up one of the old narrow turnpike stairs that connect the storeys of an Edinburgh land, or tenement-house, is one way of making contact with old Edinburgh. The stones seem to talk.

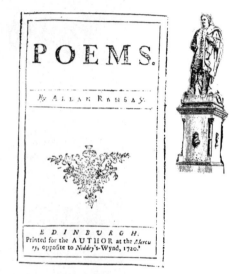

Leaving these historic courts we walk up to Castlehill, which is the final section of this Royal Mile, past Camera Obscura, to Ramsay Garden. Here is the house of Allan Ramsay who is every bit as much a poet of the Old Town as Robert Fergusson. He built his octagonal house in his old age; it was known to Edinburgh wits as the Goose-Pie. His painter son, Allan Ramsay, lived in the house after his father's death and John Galt, the novelist, here wrote much of his *Annals of the Parish*, 1821. Here it is difficult to see the house now as Ramsay Garden was built around it by Patrick Geddes whose Heritage Trail is marked by plaques throughout this part of the Old Town. A good view of Ramsay's house can be got from Princes Street, standing by his statue.

It can be convincingly argued that without Ramsay's work as an editor of anthologies of Scots poetry and as an activist for native Scottish culture we would not have the great poetry of Burns nor that of Robert Fergusson, nor that of poets of this century who have walked, as residents or visitors, the streets of the Old Town of Edinburgh and have written in a language true to themselves, whether the Scots of Lewis Spence, Hugh MacDiarmid, Robert Garioch, Sydney Goodsir Smith and many younger poets or the English of Marion Angus, Norman MacCaig, Tessa Ransford or, again, many younger poets.

Like Robert Fergusson, Allan Ramsay was a member of one of the many clubs of the Old Town. His was the Easy Club and those who knew his poetry first were his fellow members. The colloquial tone and the subjects of his poems are most suitable to such performances. One of the best poems is "Elegy on Lucky Wood in the Canongate, May 1717". His audience would be familiar with Lucky Wood as someone who greeted them as they entered her establishment. When Ramsay prepared his poems for publication he provided footnotes which his friends would not have required. So in an edition of his poems he explains, "Lucky Wood kept an alehouse in the Canongate, was much respected for her hospitality, honesty, and the neatness of both her person and her house". This elegy, with Ramsay's notes, is printed on pages 56 - 7. One verse of this poem has a reference to an Aitkenhead who often cost the drinkers at Lucky Wood's "mony a gill". In his note Ramsay introduces Aitkenhead as, "The Netherbow porter, to whom Lucky's customers were often obliged for opening the port for them, when they staid out till the small hours after midnight". So again we have a reference to the famous old Netherbow gate.

The convivial tavern life of Edinburgh revealed in the poems of Ramsay and Fergusson can be seen to continue, in a twentieth-century form, in the life and poetry of Sydney Goodsir Smith (1915-75). His masterpiece is a long love sequence entitled *Under the Eilden Tree*, see the short extract on page 68. Another very fine longer poem by Goodsir Smith is *Kynd Kittock's Land*, see page 73, and it is more firmly rooted in the Old Town,

Sydney Goodsir Smith

> Look doun there nou and see -
> See! Doun the Close at the World's End, Kynd Kittock
> Haein fun as usual in her ain sweet way
> Humped in a doorway stinko as a Bacchic maid
> - She dee'd o' drouth five hunder year sinsyne
> (But ye'll no ken o' this);

This poem not only links Goodsir Smith to the convivial poetry of Ramsay and Fergusson but also to the author of a medieval poem entitled "The Ballad of Kynd Kittock", possibly William Dunbar. The heroine of this outrageous poem was, like Ramsay's Lucky Wood, a keeper of a tavern although not quite in the Old Town of Edinburgh, as Kynd Kittock's alehouse was outside the gates of Paradise as she could not thole the respectable world within them. Well may Sydney Goodsir Smith end his *Kynd Kittock's Land* with lines that carry us out into endless and placeless time whilst also firmly placing us at the end of Edinburgh's High Street before World's End Close near to where once stood the Netherbow which also led out into the unknown,

> This is mine, Kynd Kittock's land,
> For ever and aye while stane shall stand -
> For ever and aye till the World's End.

Allan Ramsay

We began Walk 1 at the Palace of Holyroodhouse and passed World's End Close to end at St Giles. We began Walk 2 at World's End Close and ended it at the site of the Edinburgh Bedlam where Robert Fergusson died. We began this Walk 3 at World's End Close and passed St Giles to come to Ramsay Lane. From here we go to Edinburgh Castle high on Castle Rock. If the Eiffel Tower is the symbol of Paris and skyscrapers that of New York, the Castle is the symbol of Edinburgh. For many of us, however, the line of the Old Town going down from the Castle is an essential balance to the Castle. Walter Scott wrote famous lines in which Marmion looks on Edinburgh before the battle of Flodden. As a battle of defeat Flodden is a powerful symbol for all Scots as World's End Close was a symbol of the alien world out there for citizens of the Old Town of Edinburgh, including some of its poets. But Scott's lines reveal pride rather than apprehension,

Walter Scott

> Where the huge castle holds its state,
> And all the steep slope down,
> Whose ridgy back heaves to the sky,
> Piled deep and massy, close and high,
> Mine own romantic town!

Leaving Ramsay Garden and Lane we cross Castle Esplanade to enter the Castle. Our destination is the small chapel of Queen Margaret on the highest point of this Castle Rock. It is a beautiful small building, which requires silence, although I break that in a poem on page 75. Now I do not.

Leaving the Chapel and moving forward to the railings we have the panorama of northern Edinburgh far below; over the New Town, over the Forth and Fife on the opposite shore. Down in Princes Street is the grey gothic Scott Monument and to the left of that towering edifice glows the white statue of Allan Ramsay, a symbol that is positioned perfectly in this landscape. In the middle distance to the left of the green dome of the Bank of Scotland the Burns monument can be seen set off by clumps of trees. All the scene lacks is a statue of Robert Fergusson but poets live by words and not memorials in stone. And in Fergusson's words not only does *he* live but also the Old Town of Edinburgh. And many of the poets of this book would seem to agree with him, when he wrote,

> Auld Reikie! wale o' ilka town
> That Scotland kens beneath the moon.

AULD REIKIE

From AULD REIKIE

By ROBERT FERGUSSON

Auld Reikie! wale o' ilka town
That Scotland kens beneath the moon;
Whare couthy chiels at e'ening meet
Their bizzing craigs and mou's to weet:
And blythly gar auld Care gae bye
Wi' blinkit and wi' bleering eye:
O'er lang frae thee the Muse has been
Sae frisky on the simmer's green,
Whan flowers and gowans wont to glent
In bonny blinks upo' the bent;
But now the leaves a yellow die,
Peel'd frae the branches, quickly fly;
And now frae nouther bush nor brier
The spreckl'd mavis greets your ear;
Nor bonny blackbird skims and roves
To seek his love in yonder groves.
    Then Reikie, welcome! Thou canst charm
Unfleggit by the year's alarm;
Not Boreas, that sae snelly blows,
Dare here pap in his angry nose:
Thanks to our dads, whase biggin stands
A shelter to surrounding lands.
    Now morn, with bonny purpie-smiles,
Kisses the air-cock o' St. Giles;
Rakin their ein, the servant lasses
Early begin their lies and clashes;
Ilk tells her friend of saddest distress,
That still she brooks frae scouling mistress;
And wi' her joe in turnpike stair
She'd rather snuff the stinking air,
As be subjected to her tongue,
When justly censur'd in the wrong.

EARLY SUNDAY MORNING, EDINBURGH

By NORMAN MACCAIG

Crosshatch of streets: some waterfall
Down pits, some rear to lay their forepaws
On hilly ledges; others bore
Tunnels through lilac, gean and holly.

A stretch of sky makes what it can
Of ships sailing and sailing islands.
Trees open their rustling hands
And toss birds up, a fountain, a fanfare.

A yellow milkcart clipclops by
Like money shaken in a box,
Less yellow than the golden coxcomb
Gallanting on St. Giles's spire.

And people idle into space
And disappear again in it -
Apparitions from nowhere: unseen
Distances shine from their faces.

And, fore and hindpaws out of line,
And old dog mooches by, his gold
Eyes hung down below hunched shoulders
His tail switching, feathery, finely.

wale, best	glent, gleam
ilka, every	mavis, song-thrush
kens, knows	unfleggit, undismayed
couthy chiels,	snelly, sharply
sociable fellows	biggin, building
gar, cause	purpie-smiles, blushes
gowans, daisies	ein, eye

Auld Reikie, is the old familiar name for Edinburgh
which for centuries was overhung with reik (smoke).

There are references to Fergusson, truly a poet of
Edinburgh, throughout the walks.
For St Giles see pages 14 - 16.
For Norman MacCaig see page 25.

WINTER SUNSET IN EDINBURGH

By TESSA RANSFORD

The sunset at teatime is everywhere:
it gets in under averted eyes,
strays between grey thicknesses
of cloud,
in and out of branches and chimneys,
dashes itself against windows and walls
and plays with children
on their way home from school.

The sunset is like a bright old lady
who puts on her old-fashioned finery
and makes a sudden sortie to
the library;
in and out of acquaintances and friends,
dashes her smiles against strangers and dogs,
and chats to children
on their way home from school.

From ILLE TERRARUM

By ROBERT LOUIS STEVENSON

But noo the auld city, street by street,
An' winter fu' o' snaw an' sleet,
Awhile shut in my gangrel feet
        An' goavin' mettle;
Noo is the soopit ingle sweet,
        An' liltin' kettle.

An' noo the winter winds complain;
Cauld lies the glaur in ilka lane;
Our draigled hizzie, tautit wean
        An' drucken lads,
In the mirk nicht, the winter rain
        Dribbles an' blads.

Whan bugles frae the Castle rock,
An' beaten drums wi' dowie shock,
Wauken, at cauld-rife sax o'clock,
        My chitterin' frame,
I mind me on the kintry cock,
        The kintry hame.

I mind me on yon bonnie bield;
An' Fancy traivels far afield
To gaither a' that gairdens yield
        O' sun an' Simmer:
To hearten up a dowie chield,
        Fancy's the limmer!

gangrel, vagrant
goavin', staring
soopit, swept
glaur, mud
draigled, bedraggled
tautit, ragged
wean, child
mirk, dark
blads, splashes
dowie, sad
cauld-rife, chilly
chitterin, shivering
kintry, country
beild, shelter
chield, chap
limmer, flirt

For Tessa Ransford see page 12.
For Robert Louis Stevenson see page 15.

From EDINBURGH

By HUGH MACDIARMID

Most of the denizens wheeze, sniffle,
and exude a sort of snozzling whnoff whnoff,
apparently through a hydrophile sponge.
Ezra Pound

The capital of Scotland is called Auld Reekie,
Signifying a monstrous acquiescence
In the domination of the ends
By the evidences of effort.
- Not the mastery of matter
By the spirit of man
But, at best, a damnable draw,
A division of the honours
And, far more, the dishonours!
- Dark symbol of a society
of "dog eat dog".
Under which the people reveal themselves to
    the world
Completely naked in their own skin,
Like toads!

Yes, see, the dead snatch at the living here.
So the social corpse, the dead class,
The dead mode of life, the dead religion,
Have an after life as vampires.
They are not still in their graves
But return among us.
They rise with the fumes
From the chimney of the crematorium
And again settle down on the earth
And cover it with black filth.

For MacDiarmid see pages 19 and 20.

EDINBURGH
Midnight

By HUGH MACDIARMID

Glasgow is null,
Its suburbs shadows
And the Clyde a cloud.

Dundee is dust
And Aberdeen a shell.

But Edinburgh is a mad god's dream,
Fitful and dark,
Unseizable in Leith
And wildered by the Forth,
But irresistibly at last
Cleaving to sombre heights
Of passionate imagining
Til stonily,
From soaring battlements,
Earth eyes Eternity.

Hugh MacDiarmid

The Palace of
Holyroodhouse
in the nineteenth
century.

TO HOLYROODHOUSE

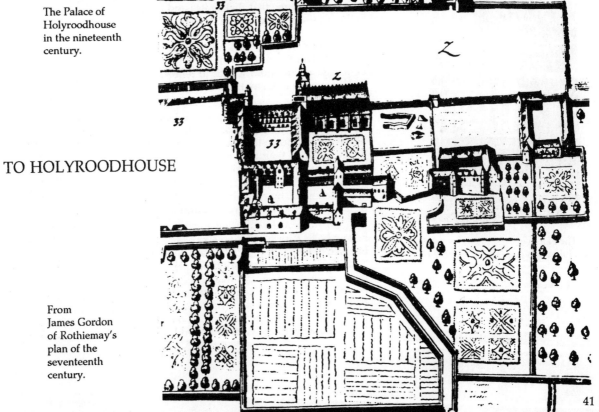

From
James Gordon
of Rothiemay's
plan of the
seventeenth
century.

From AULD REIKIE

By ROBERT FERGUSSON

Or shou'd some canker'd biting show'r
The day and a' her sweets deflour,
To Holy-rood-house let me stray,
And gie to musing a' the day;
Lamenting what auld Scotland knew,
Bien days for ever frae her view:
O Hamilton, for shame! the Muse
Would pay to thee her couthy vows,
Gin ye wad tent the humble strain,
And gie's our dignity again:
For O, waes me! the thistle springs
In domicile of ancient kings,
Without a patriot to regrete
Our palace, and our ancient state.

The Palace of
Holyroodhouse

TO THE QUEEN

By LORD DARNLEY

Be governour baith guid and gratious;
Be leill and luifand to thy liegis all;
Be large of fredome and no thing desyrous;
Be just to pure for ony thing may fall;
Be ferme of faith and constant as ane wall;
Be reddye evir to stanche evill and discord;
Be cheretabill, and sickerlye thou sall
Be bowsum ay to knaw thy God and Lord.

Be nocht to proud of wardlie guidis heir;
Be weill bethocht thai will remane na tyde;
Be sicker als that thou man die but weir;
Be war thairwith the tyme will no man byde.
Be vertewus and set all vyce on syde;
Be patient, lawlie and misericord;
Be rewlit so quhairevir thou go or byde;
Be bowsum ay to knaw thy God and Lord.

Be weill avysit of quhome thow counsale tais;
Be sewer of thame that thai be leill and trew;
Bethink the als quhidder thai be freindis, or fais.
Be to thy saull, thair sawis or thou persew:
Be nevir our hastye to wirk and syne to rew;
Be nocht thair freind that makis the fals record;
Be reddye evir all guid workis to renew;
Be bowsum ay to knaw thy God and Lord.

Be traist and conquese thy awin heretage
Be ennemyes of auld now occupyit;
Be strenth and force thou sobir thai man swage
Be law of God - thair may no man deny it;
Be nocht as lantern in mirknes unspyit;
Be thou in rycht thi landis suld be restored,
Be wirschop so thy name beis magnefeit;
Be bowsum ay to knaw thy God and Lord.

Be to rebellis strong as lyoun eik;
Be ferce to follow thame quhairevir thai found;
Be to thy liegemen bayth soft and meik;
Be thair succour and help thame haill and sound;
Be knaw thy cure and caus quhy thow was cround;
Be besye evir that justice be nocht smord;
Be blyith in hart; thir wordis oft expound;
Be bowsum ay to knaw thy God and Lord.

Mary Queen of Scots

bien, prosperous

pure, poor people
sickerlie, surely
bowsum, tractable
guidis, goods
sicker, sure
thou man, thou must
weir, doubt
sawis, words
wirk, act
swage, assuage
nocht, nothing
mirkness, darkness
eik, any, each
smord, smouthered

For the Palace of
Holyroodhouse
see pages 7-9.
For Darnley see pages 8,
12 and 18-19.

ALAS! POOR QUEEN

By MARION ANGUS

She was skilled in music and the dance
And the old arts of love
At the court of the poisoned rose
And the perfumed glove,
And gave her beautiful hand
To the pale Dauphin
A triple crown to win -
And she loved little dogs
      And parrots
        And red-legged partridges
And the golden fishes of the Duc de Guise
And a pigeon with a blue ruff
She had from Monsieur d'Elboeuf.

Master John Knox was no friend to her;
She spoke him soft and kind,
Her honeyed words were Satan's lure
The unwary soul to bind.
"Good sir, doth a lissome shape
And a comely face
Offend your God His Grace
Whose Wisdom maketh these
Golden fishes of the Duc de Guise?"

She rode through Liddesdale with a song:
"Ye streams sae wondrous strang,
Oh, mak' me a wrack as I come back
But spare me as I gang."
While a hill-bird cried and cried
Like a spirit lost
By the grey storm-wind tost.

Consider the way she had to go.
Think of the hungry snare,
The net she herself had woven,
Aware or unaware,
Of the dancing feet grown still,
The blinded eyes -

Queens should be cold and wise,
And she loved little things,
      Parrots
        And red-legged partridges
And the golden fishes of the Duc de Guise
And the pigeon with the blue ruff
She had from Monsieur d'Elboeuf.

John Knox

Mary was for a time Queen of
France as well as Queen of Scots.
Mary of Guise was James V's
second wife and mother of
Mary Queen of Scots.
For Knox and Mary see page 12.
For Mary see also page 8.

Mary of Guise

43

MARIE HAMILTON
(Anonymous)

Marie Hamilton 's to the kirk gane,
  Wi ribbons in her hair;
The king thought mair o Marie Hamilton
  Than ony that were there.

Marie Hamilton 's to the kirk gane,
  Wi ribbons on her breast;
The king thought mair o Marie Hamilton
  Then he listend to the priest.

Marie Hamilton 's to the kirk gane,
  Wi gloves upon her hands;
The king thocht mair o Marie Hamilton,
  Than the queen and a' her lands.

She hadna been about the king's court
  A month, but barely one,
Till she was beloved by a' the king's court,
  And the king the only man.

He's courted her in the kitchen,
  He's courted her in the ha,
He's courted her in the laigh cellar,
  And that was warst of a'.

Doun then cam the auld queen,
  Goud tassels tying her hair:
"O Marie, where's the bonny wee babe
  That I heard greet sae sair?"

She hadna been about the king's court
  A month, but barely three,
Till frae the king's court Marie Hamilton,
  Marie Hamilton durstna be.

The king is to the Abbey gane,
  To pu the Abbey-tree,
To scale the babe frae Marie's hairt,
  But the thing it wadna be.

She's rowd it in her apron
  And she's thrown it in the sea;
Says, "Sink ye, swim ye, bonny wee babe!
  You'l neer get mair o me."

Word's gane to the kitchen,
  And word's gane to the ha,
That Marie Hamilton gangs wi bairn
  To the hichest Stewart of a'.

"There never was a babe intill my room,
  As little designs to be;
It was but a touch o my sair side,
  Come oer my fair bodie."

"O Marie, put on your robes o black,
  Or else your robes o broun,
For ye maun gang wi me the nicht,
  To see fair Edinbro toun."

"I winna put on my robes o black,
  Nor yet my robes of broun;
But I'll put on my robes o white,
  To shine through Edinbro toun."

When she gaed up the Cannongate,
  She laugh'd loud laughters three;
But whan she cam doun the Cannongate
  The tear blinded her ee.

Canongate Tolbooth

laigh, low
rowd, wrapped
ee, eye.

See pages 12 and 14.

The Palace of
Holyroodhouse
as it was before
the fire of 1650,
after Gordon
of Rothiemay.

When she cam to the Netherbow Port,
 She laughed loud laughters three;
But when she cam to the gallows-foot,
 The tears blinded her ee.

When she gaed up the Tolbooth stair,
 The heel cam aff her shee;
And lang or she cam down again
 She was condemnd to dee.

When she cam doun the Cannogate,
 The Cannogate sae free,
Many a ladie lookd oer her window,
 Weeping for this ladie.

"Ye need nae weep for me," she says,
 "Ye need nae weep for me;
For had I not slain mine own sweet babe,
 This death I wadna dee.

"Bring me a bottle of wine," she says,
 "The best that eer ye hae,
That I may drink to my weil-wishers,
 And they may drink to me.

"Here's a health to the jolly sailors,
 That sail upon the sea;
Let them never let on to my faither and mither
 That I cam here to dee.

"Oh little did my mither think,
 The day she cradled me,
What lands I was to traivel through,
 What daith I was to dee.

"Oh little did my faither think,
 The day he held up me
What lands I was to traivel through,
 What daith I was to dee.

"Last nicht I washd the queen's feet,
 And gently laid her doun;
And a' the thanks I've gotten the nicht
 To be hangd in Edinbro toun!

"Last nicht there was four Maries,
 The nicht there 'l be but three;
There was Marie Seton, and Marie Beton,
 And Marie Carmichael, and me."

PALATIVM REGIVM EDINENSE
quod & Cænobium S. Crucis

THE QUEEN'S BATH-HOUSE, HOLYROOD

By LEWIS SPENCE

Time that has dinged doun castels and hie toures,
And cast great crouns like tinsel in the fire,
That halds his hand for palace nor for byre,
Stands sweir at this, the oe of Venus' boures.
Not Time himself can dwall withouten floures,
Though aiks maun fa' the rose sall bide entire;
So sall this diamant of a queen's desire
Outflourish all the stanes that Time devours.

Mony a strength his turret-heid sall tine
Ere this sall fa' whare a queen lay in wine,
Whose lamp was her ain lily flesh and star.
The walls of luve the mair triumphant are
Gif luve were waesome habiting that place;
Luve has maist years that has a murning face.

PORTRAIT OF MARY STUART, HOLYROOD

By LEWIS SPENCE

Wauken be nicht, and bydand on some boon,
    Glamour of saul, or spirituall grace,
    I haf seen sancts and angells in the face,
And like a fere of seraphy the moon;
But in nae mirk nor sun-apparelled noon
    Nor pleasance of the planets in their place
    Of luve devine haf seen sae pure a trace
As in yon shadow of the Scottis croun.

Die not, O rose, dispitefull of hir mouth,
    Nor be ye lillies waeful at hir snaw;
        This dim devyce is but hir painted sake,
The mirour of ane star of vivand youth,
    That not hir velvets nor hir balas braw
        Can oueradorn, or luve mair luvely make.

QUEEN OF SCOTS

By NORMAN MACCAIG

Mary was depressed.
She hadn't combed her red hair yet.
She hadn't touched her frightful Scottish breakfast.
Her lady-in-waiting, another Mary,
had told Rizzio Her Majesty wasn't at home,
a lie so obvious it was another way
of telling the truth.

Mary was depressed.
She wanted real life and here she was
acting in a real play, with real blood in it.

And she thought of the years to come
and of the frightful plays that would be written
about the play she was in.

She said something in French
and with her royal foot she kicked
the spaniel that was gazing at her
with exophthalmic adoration.

dinged, smashed
sweir, reluctant
oe, grandchild
aiks, oaks
tine, lose
waesome, woesome
fere, companion
mirk, darkness

For Mary at Holyrood see page 8.
For Rizzio see page 8.

Queen Mary's Bath-house

From ANE NEW YEAR GIFT TO QUEEN MARY WHEN SHE FIRST CAME HAME, 1562

By ALEXANDER SCOTT

Welcome, illustrat Lady, and our Queen!
Welcome, our lion with the Fleur-de-lyce!
Welcome, our thristle with the Lorraine green!
Welcome, our rubent rose upon the ryce!
Welcome, our gem and joyful genetryce!
Welcome, our beill of Albion to beir!
Welcome, our pleasand Princess maist of price!
God give thee grace aganis this guid new year.

This guid new year, we hope, with grace of God,
Sail be of peax, tranquility, and rest;
This year sall richt and reason rule the rod,
Whilk sa lang season has been sore suppressed;
This year firm faith sall freely be confessed,
And all erroneous questions put arrear;
To labour that this life amang us lest
God give thee grace aganis this guid new year.

Herefore address thee duly to decoir
And rule thy reign with hie magnificence;
Begin at God to gar set furth his gloir,
And of his gospel get experience;
Cause his true Kirk by had in reverence;
So sall thy name and fame spread far and near;
Now, this thy dett to do with diligence,
God give thee grace against this guid new year.

illustrat, illustrious
rubent, ruby
ryce, spray
genetryce, mother
aganis, to meet
decoir, adorn
gloir, glory
dett, duty

From FORTH FEASTING

A PANEGYRICKE TO THE KINGS MOST EXCELLENT MAJESTY

By WILLIAM DRUMMOND

What blustring Noise now interrupts my Sleepe?
What echoing Shouts thus cleave my chrystal Deep?
And call mee hence from out my watrie Court?
What Melodie, what Sounds of Joy and Sport,
Bee these heere hurl'd from ev'rie neighbour Spring?
With what lowd Rumours doe the Mountaines ring?
Which in unusuall Pompe on tip-toes stand,
And (full of Wonder) over-looke the Land?
Whence come these glittring Throngs, these Meteors bright
This golden People set unto my Sight?
Whence doth this Praise, Applause, and Love, arise?
What Load-starre east-ward draweth thus all Eyes?
Am I awake? or have some Dreames conspir'd
To mocke my Sense with Shadowes much desir'd?
Stare I that living Face, see I those Lookes,
Which with Delight wont to amaze my Brookes?
Doe I behold that Worth, that Man divine,
This Ages Glorie, by these Bankes of mine?
Then is it true what long I wish'd in vaine?
That my much-loving Prince is come againe?

Load-starre, guiding star,
   the pole star

For Alexander Scott
(c. 1515 - c. 1583)
see page 8.
Drummond's poem was
addressed to James VI when
he returned
to Edinburgh in 1617.
See pages 8-9.

SONNET

By JAMES VI

All kinde of wronge allace it now aboundes
And honestie is fleemed out of this land;
Now trumprie ouer trueth his triumphe soundes;
Who now can knowe the hart by tongue or hand?
Cummes ever justice at the barre to stand?
Where can she be in these our later dayes?
Alike in water for to wagg a wande
As speare for her if truelie sundrie sayes,
For manie now abroade doe daylie blaize
That justice hath her hart infected sore.
How can she then be cleane in anie wayes
Bot must become corrupted more and more?
Sume lockman now hath locked up apart
Poore justice, martyr'd with a meschant hart.

SONNET

By ALEXANDER MONTGOMERIE

Remembers thou in Aesope of a taill?
A loving dog wes of his maister fane;
To fawn on him wes all his pastym haill.
His courteous maister clappit him agane.
By stood ane asse, a beist of blunter brane.
Perceiving this, bot looking to no freet,
To pleis hir maister with the counterpane,
Sho clambe on him with hir foull clubbit feet,
To play the messan thoght sho wes not meit.
Sho meinit weill I grant; hir mynd wes guid,
Bot whair sho troude hir maister suld hir treit,
They battound hir whill that they saw hir bluid.
So stands with me, who loves with all my hairt
My maister best; some taks it in ill pairt.

wagg a wande, wave a stick
speare, ask
meschant, miserable
freet, omen
counterpane, like
messan, lap-dog

For James VI see pages 8-9.
For Montgomerie see page 8.

CAT AND KING

By ALEXANDER SCOTT
(1920 - 1989)

A cat may look at a king
   - Oh, fairly that!
But a king can swack the heid
   Frae onie cat.

The heid may look at a king
   Wi gloweran een
- But whatever 's the guid o thon
   Whan naething 's seen?

The Knowing
One

swack the heid, swipe the
   head
gloweran een, scowling eyes
guid o thon, good of that

tunder, tinder
Tramontane, the pole star,
   the guiding light.
Supercheries, frauds
beagling Marmosets, spying
   monkeys.

For Charles I see pages 13 and 15.

From THE ENTERTAINMENT of the High and Mighty Monarch, Prince Charles King of great Brittaine, France and Ireland, into his ancient and Royall Citie of Edenbourgh, the 15 of June 1633.

By WILLIAM DRUMMOND

[The King is greeted by various tableaux on his way into the city; and is addressed by Caledonia, the Muses, a selection of classical deities, and the sun and the moon.]

JOVE

Delight of heaven, sole honour of the earth,
Jove (courting thine ascendant) at thy birth
Proclaimed thee a King, and made it true,
That Emperies should to thy worth be due,
He gave thee what was good, and what was great,
What did belong to love, and what to state,
Rare gifts whose ardors turne the hearts of all,
Like tunder when flint attomes on it fall;
The *Tramontane* which thy faire course directs,
Thy counsells shall approve by their effects;
Justice kept low by grants, and wrongs, and jarres,
Thou shalt relieve, and crowne with glistering starres,
Whom nought save law of force could keepe in awe
Thou shalt turne Clients to the force of law,
Thou armes shalt brandish for thine owne defence,
Wrongs to repell, and guard weake innocence,
Which to thy last effort thou shalt uphold,
As Oake the Ivy which it doth infold;
All overcome, at last thy selfe orecome,
Thou shalt make passion yield to reasons doome:
For smiles of fortune shall not raise thy mind,
Nor dismall most disasters turne declin'd,
True *Honour* shall reside within thy Court,
Sobrietie, and *Truth* there still resort,
Keepe promis'd faith thou shalt, Supercheries
Detest, and beagling Marmosets despise,
Thou, others to make rich, shalt not make poore
Thy selfe, but give that thou mayst still give more;

From THE SONG OF JENNY GEDDES

By JOHN STUART BLACKIE

Some praise the fair Queen Mary, and some the good Queen Bess,
And some the wise Aspasia, beloved by Pericles;
But o'er the world's brave women, there's one that bears the rule,
The valiant Jenny Geddes, that flung the three legged stool.
With a row-dow - at them now! - Jenny flung the stool.

'Twas the twenty-third of July, in the sixteen thirty-seven,
On the Sabbath morn from high St. Giles the solemn peal was given;
King Charles had sworn that Scottish men should pray by printed rule;
He sent a book, but never dreamt of danger from a stool.
With a row-dow - yes, I trow - there's danger in a stool!

The Council and the Judges, with ermined pomp elate,
The Provost and the Bailies in gold and crimson state,
Fair silken-vested ladies, grave doctors of the school,
Were there to please the King, and learn the virtues of a stool.
With a row-dow - yes, I trow! - there's virtue in a stool!

The Bishop and the Dean came in wi' muckle gravity,
Right smooth and sleek, but lordly pride was lurking in their e'e;
Their full lawn sleeves were blown and big, like seals in briny pool;
They bore a book, but little thought they soon should feel a stool.
With a row-dow - yes!, I trow! they'll feel a three-legged stool!

The Dean he to the altar went, and, with a solemn look,
He cast his eyes to heaven, and read the curious-printed book:
In Jenny's heart the blood upwelled with bitter anguish full;
Sudden she started to her legs, and stoutly grasped the stool!
With a row-dow! - at them now!- firmly grasped the stool!

As when a mountain wild-cat springs upon a rabbit small,
So Jenny on the Dean springs, with gush of holy gall;
Wilt thou say mass at my lugs, thou popish-puling fool?
No! no! she said, and at his head she flung the three-legged stool.
With a row-dow - at them now! - Jenny fling the stool!

For Blackie see pages 15 and 32.
For Jenny Geddes
see page 15.

50

JAMES GRAHAM
MARQUIS OF MONTROSE

HIS METRICAL VOW
(On the Death of Charles I)

Great, Good and Just, could I but rate
My Grief to Thy too Rigid Fate!
I'd weep the World in such a Strain,
As it would once deluge again:
But since Thy loud-tongu'd Blood demands Supplies,
More from *Briareus* Hands, than *Argus* Eyes,
I'll tune Thy Elegies to Trumpet-sounds,
And write Thy Epitaph in Blood and Wounds!

HIS METRICAL PRAYER
(On the Eve of his own Execution)

Let them bestow on ev'ry Airth a Limb;
Open all my Veins, that I may swim
To Thee my Saviour, in that Crimson Lake;
Then place my pur-boil'd Head upon a Stake;
Scatter my Ashes, throw them in the Air:
Lord (since Thou know'st where all these Atoms are)
I'm hopeful, once Thou'lt recollect my Dust,
And confident Thou'lt raise me with the Just.

See page 16.

Lawnmarket

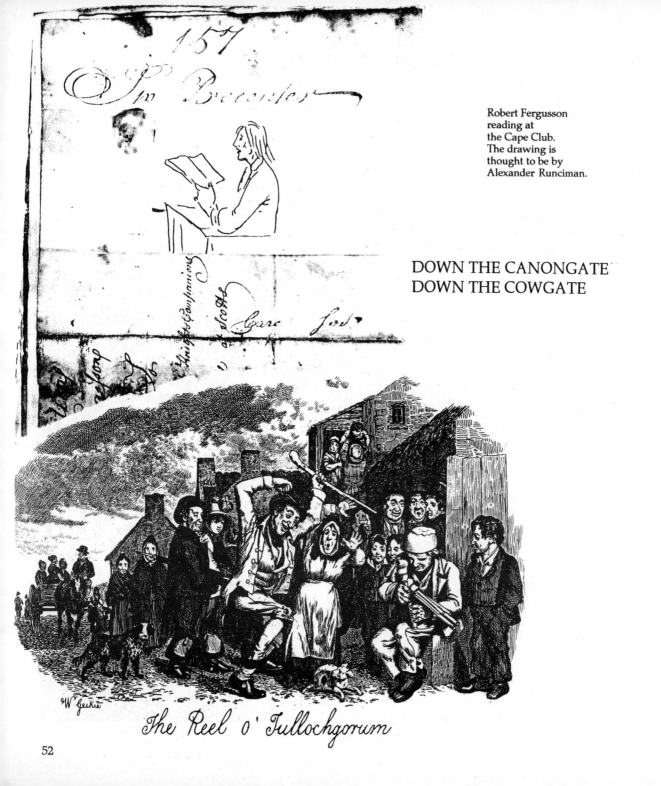

Robert Fergusson
reading at
the Cape Club.
The drawing is
thought to be by
Alexander Runciman.

DOWN THE CANONGATE
DOWN THE COWGATE

The Reel o' Tullochgorum

EPITAPH
HERE LIES
ROBERT FERGUSSON
POET
Born, September 5th, 1751
Died 16th October, 1774

By ROBERT BURNS

No sculptur'd marble here, nor pompous lay,
'No story'd urn nor animated bust;'
This simple stone directs pale SCOTIA's way.
To pour her sorrows o'er her POET's dust.

See pages 9 and 32.
The date of Fergusson's birth
should be 1750.

AT ROBERT FERGUSSON'S
GRAVE
October 1962

By ROBERT GARIOCH

Canongait kirkyaird in the failing year
is auld and grey, the wee roseirs are bare;
five gulls leam white agin the dirty air:
why are they here? There's naething for them here.

Why are we here oursels? We gaither near
the grave. Fergusons mainly, quite a fair
turn-out, respectfu, ill at ease, we stare
at daith - there's an address - I canna hear.

Aweill, we staund bareheidit in the haar,
murnin a man that gaed back til the pool
twa-hunner year afore our time. The glaur

that haps his banes glowres back. Strang, present dool
ruggs at my hairt. Lichtlie this gin ye daur:
here Robert Burns knelt and kissed the mool.

roseirs, rose-bushes	glaur, mud
leam, flame	dool, grief, sorrow
haar, sea-mist	ruggs, drags
	gin, if
	mool, soil for a grave

From TO ROBERT FERGUSSON

By ROBERT GARIOCH

A conter, we've some rotten riggin
of ratton-eaten Cougait biggin
that heard langsyne the skeelie jiggin
    of your new verse.
Hard-pressed, I wale yon airt to dig in
    and micht dae worse.

Our life's a bogle-hauntit dream
owre thrang wi wirrikows to seem
quite real; our fun a fireflaucht-gleam
    whang'd throu a nicht
of gurliewhirkies huge and breme,
    loppert wi fricht.

Ye gaed about in guid braid claith
wi fient a thocht of want or skaith,
in howffs at hy-jinks never laith
    to blaw your chanter,
syne in cursed Darien's bedlam, Daith
    wrocht your mishanter.

             * * *

Aweill, ye're deid, gey lang sinsyne -
the Scottish elegiac line
I'll spare ye, tho, as ye ken fine,
    ye scrievit monie
crouse stanzas whan ye'd cam to tine
    some decent cronie.

My ain toun's makar, monie an airt
formed us in common, faur apairt
in time, but fell alike in hert;
    I whiles forget
that ye ligg there ablow the clart
    of Canogait.

             * * *

The auld High Schule (gane Royal syne)
your Alma Mater was and mine,
and whar ye construed, line by line,
    the Gallic Weirs
we ken the airt, doun by the Wynd
    of the Black Friars.

The wind that blaws frae Nor to South,
skirlan frae ilka close's mouth,
has nithert baith o's in our youth
    and coupt us, whiles,
as we gaed hame wi slockent drouth
    doun by Sanct Giles'.

But aye we'd rise wi little hairm
and cleik ilk ither by the airm
singan in unison to chairm
    awa the skaith,
syne seek some cantraip, harum-skarum
    and naething laith.

Darien, the workhouse, in the
Bedlam of which Fergusson died, see
pages 22 and 23.

For High School see page 25.

ratten-eaten, rat-eaten
biggin, building
skeelie, skilful
bogle-hauntit,
    apparition-haunted
thrang, busy
wirrikows, frightful objects
fire-flaucht, lightning flash
whanged, wip-lashed
gurliewhirkies, nameless terrors
breme, furious
loppert, coagulated
fient a thocht, devil a thought
skaith, harm
howffs, inns
hy-jinks, a drinking game,
    drinking by lot
syne, then
wrocht, worked
gey lang sinsyne, very long ago
ken, know
scrievit, wrote
crouse, lively
tine, lose
makar, poet
airt, direction
ligg, lie
clart, mud
cleik, hook
skaith, danger
cantraip, charm
laith, loath

THE DAFT-DAYS

By ROBERT FERGUSSON

mirk, dark
dowie, gloomy
glours, looks sternly
dwyning, declining
canty, cheerful
bield, shelter
caldrife, spiritless
gar, make
scantlins, scarcely
kickshaws, novelties
fairn-year, last year
browster wives, female ale-sellers
reaming, creaming
roset, rub with resin.
capernoity, whimsical,
    ill-natured

Daft-Days, the holidays at New
Year (Yule, Hogmanay, New
Year's Day and Handsel Monday,
the first Monday of the New
Year).

Tullochgorum is a tune that was
given words by John Skinner.
"Vile Italian tricks" is an
objection to the distortion
of native Scots songs by
artificial over-elaboration
in the Italian style.

For City Guard see
pages 20-21, 22 and 27.

Now mirk December's dowie face
Glours our the rigs wi' sour grimace,
While, thro' his *minimum* of space,
                The bleer-ey'd sun,
Wi' blinkin light and stealing pace,
                His race doth run.

From naked groves nae birdie sings;
To shepherd's pipe nae hillock rings;
The breeze nae od'rous flavour brings
                From Borean cave;
And dwyning Nature droops her wings,
                Wi' visage grave.

Mankind but scanty pleasure glean
Frae snawy hill or barren plain,
Whan Winter, 'midst his nipping train,
                Wi' frozen spear,
Sends drift owr a' his bleak domain,
                And guides the weir.

Auld Reikie! thou'rt the canty hole,
A bield for mony caldrife soul,
Wha snugly at thine ingle loll,
                Baith warm and couth;
While round they gar the bicker roll
                To weet their mouth.

When merry Yule-day comes, I trow,
You'll scantlins find a hungry mou;
Sma' are our cares, our stamacks fou
                O' gusty gear,
And kickshaws, strangers to our view,
                Sin fairn-year.

Ye browster wives, now busk ye bra,
And fling your sorrows far awa';
Then, come and gies the tither blaw
                Of reaming ale,
Mair precious than the well of Spa,
                Our hearts to heal.

Then tho' at odds wi' a' the warl',
Amang oursells we'll never quarrel;
Tho' Discord gie a canker'd snarl
                To spoil our glee,
As lang's there's pith into the barrel
                We'll drink and 'gree.

Fidlers, your pins in temper fix,
And roset weel your fiddlesticks,
But banish vile Italian tricks
                From out your *quorum*,
Nor *fortes* wi' *pianos* mix,
                Gie's *Tulloch Gorum*.

For nought can cheer the heart sae weil
As can a canty Highland reel;
It even vivifies the heel
                To skip and dance:
Lifeless is he wha canna feel
                Its influence.

Let mirth abound, let social cheer
Invest the dawning of the year;
Let blithesome innocence appear
                To crown our joy;
Nor envy wi' sarcastic sneer,
                Our bliss destroy.

And thou, great god of *Aqua Vitae!*
Wha sways the empire of this city,
When fou we're sometimes capernoity,
                Be thou prepar'd
To hedge us frae that black banditti,
                The City-Guard.

ELEGY ON LUCKY WOOD
IN THE CANONGATE, MAY 1717

By ALLAN RAMSAY

O Cannigate! Poor elritch hole!
What loss, what crosses does thou thole!
London and Death gars thee look drole,
        And hing thy head:
Wow, but thou has e'en a cauld coal
        To blaw indeed.

Hear me ye hills and every glen,
Ilk craig, ilk cleugh and hollow den,
And echo shrill, that a' may ken
        The waefou thud,
Be rackless Death, wha came unsenn
        To Lucky Wood.

She's dead o'er true, she's dead and gane,
Left us and Willie burd alane,
To bleer and greet, to sob and mane,
        And rugg our hair,
Because we'll ne'r see her again
        For evermair.

She gae'd as fait as a new prin,
And kept her housie snod and been;
Her peuther glanc'd upo' your een
        Like siller plate;
She was a donsie wife and clean,
        Without debate.

It did ane good to see her stools,
Her boord, fire-side and facing tools;
Rax, chandlers, tangs, and fire-shools,
        Basket wi' bread.
Poor facers now may chew pea-hools,
        Since Lucky's dead.

She ne'er gae in a lawin fause,
Nor stoups a froath aboon the hause,
Nor kept dow'd tip within her waw's,
        But reaming swats;
She never ran sour jute, because
        It gee's the batts.

She had the gate sae well to please,
With *gratis* beef, dry fish, or cheese;
Which kept our purses ay at ease,
        And health in tift,
And lent her fresh nine gallon trees
        A hearty lift.

She ga'e us aft hail legs o' lamb,
And did nae hain her mutton ham;
Then ay at Yule, when e'er we came,
        A bra' goose pye,
And was na that good belly baum?
        Nane dare deny.

The Writer lads fow well may mind her,
Furthy was she, her luck design'd her
Their common mither, sure nane kinder
        Ever brake bread;
She has na left her make behind her,
        But now she's dead.

To the sma' hours we aft sat still,
Nick'd round our toasts and snishing mill;
Good cakes we wanted ne'r at will,
        The best of bread,
Which often cost us mony a gill,
        To Aikenhead.

elritch, unearthly
thole, bear
gars, makes
ilk, every
cleugh, den between rocks
ken, know
waefou, woeful
rackless, careless
burd alane, solitary
bleer, dim the eyes
mane, moan
rugg, pull
fait, neat
prin, pin
snod and been, neat
peuther, pewter
een, eyes
donsie, clean when applied
   to any little person
ane, one
boord, table
pea-hools, pea-pods
lawen fause, false reckoning
stoups, flagons
hause, throat
dow'd tip, dead cheap ale
reaming, creaming
sour jute, sour or dead liquor
batts, colic
gate, way
tift, good order
trees, barrels
baum, comfort
writer, clerks, lawyers
furthy, forward
snishing mill, snuff mill

See page 34.

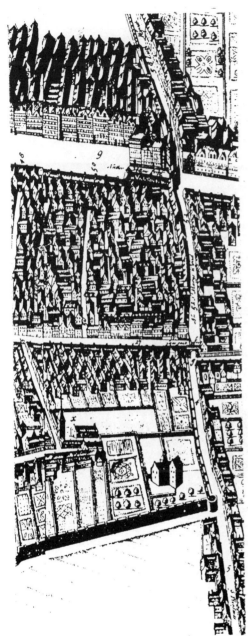

Cou'd our saut tears like Clyde, down rin,
And had we cheeks like Corra's Lin,
That a' the warld might hear the din
   Rair frae ilk head;
She was the wale of a' her kin,
   But now she's dead.

O Lucky Wood, 'tis hard to bear
The loss; but Oh! we maun forbear:
Yet sall thy memory be dear
   While blooms a tree,
And after ages bairns will spear
   'Bout thee and me.

Allan Ramsay's house

These notes are Ramsay's as are some of the glosses.
See pages 9, 13, 22, 27 and 34-5.

Lucky Wood kept an ale-house in the Canongate, was much respected for hospitality, honesty, and the neatness of her person and house.

London and Death. The place of her residence being the greatest sufferer, by the loss of our Members of Parliament, which London now enjoys, many of them having their houses there, being the suburb of Edinburgh nearest the King's palace: this with the death of Lucky Wood are sufficient to make the place ruinous.

Came unsenn: or unsent for. There's nothing extraordinary in this, it being his common custom, except in some few instances of late since the falling of the Bubbles.

Willie. Her husband William Wood.

Facing tools. Stoups (or pots) and cups, so called from the *facers*

Poor facers. The facers were a club of fair drinkers who inclined rather to spend a shilling on ale than twopence for meat. They had their name from a rule they observed of obliging themselves to throw all they left in the cup in their own faces; wherefore to save their face and cloaths they prudently sucked the liquor clean out.

She ne'er gae in, &c. All this verse is a fine picture of an honest ale-seller; a rarity.

To *Aikenhead's.* The Nether-Bow porter, to whom Lucky's customers were often obliged for opening the port for them, when they staid out till the small hours after midnight.

Like Corra's Lin. A very high precipice nigh Lanerk, over which the River of Clyde falls, making a great noise which is heard some miles off.

saut, salt
the wale, the best
spear, ask

Cowgate near the foot of Libberton Wynd

OLD EDINBURGH

By NORMAN MACCAIG

Down the Canongate
down the Cowgate
go vermilion dreams
snake's tongues of bannerets
trumpets with words from their mouths
saying *Praise me, praise me.*

Up the Cowgate
up the Canongate
lice on the march
tar on the amputated stump
Hell speaking with the tongue of Heaven
a woman tied to the tail of a cart.

And history leans by a dark entry
with words from his mouth
that say *Pity me, pity me*
but never forgive.

COUGAIT REVISITED

By DONALD CAMPBELL

"Aa ony o us ever wantit was a hoose in
Jeffrey Street." - Old lady, reminiscing
on her life in the Cougait.

Moving among sic stanes, I ken
I canna bide lang. I dinna mind
a time I wasna scunnered by this street
and I downa. Gin I could meet it
with a steady gaze for mair nor twa
three minutes at a time, I'd be gaffer
of that gang that's cawin it doun,
full of speiring wonder and a cowking disgust.

But I have no speiring now, no arguments,
no wonder. I hang about
thae black auld lands and dander owre
thae clairty gutters;
take a measure, make a count
of all the sinners, saints and ghaists
that dern ahint the snibbed and lockit shutters
time put up. And history for me
bides in nae dark entry, but maun forever
dree its kenless weird in the bonnier slums
of Burdiehouse, Gilmerton or even
a heich top-flat in the Dumbiedykes.

For hardly a soul of us ever won to Jeffrey Street.

sic, such
bide, stay
scunnered, disgusted, sickened
gin, if
speiring, questioning
cowking, retching
dander, stroll
clairty, filthy
dern ahint, hide behind
snibbed, fastened
dree, endure
kenless weird, unknown world
heich, high

For Cowgate see pages 25-6.
For Jeffrey Street see page 10.

BLACKFRIARS WYND
By DONALD CAMPBELL

A man can aye be miserable
and never ken the truth.
He'll be cheery, irresponsible
while living hand to mouth!
If his life seems in a guddle
but he hardly seems to mind -
Oh, it's ten to one he's living here
in Blackfriars Wynd!

Women whiles can be content
with the lowest of the low!
They'll be wasted, near demented
yet they'll never guess it's so!
Though they see destruction coming
to sic a likelihood they're blind -
They're just lucky to be living here
in Blackfriars Wynd!

It's the same the haill world over
and in every day and age.
While there's some that live in clover,
others trauchle for a wage.
If ye dinna ken the difference
as ye thole your daily grind -
then ye micht as well be living here
in Blackfriars Wynd!

We're the children of the closes!
We're the children of defeat!
At the mercy of the bosses
biding here in our ain street
waiting for the day that's coming
when the world wakes up to find
that there's millions of us living here
in Blackfriars Wynd!

Blackfriars Wynd!
Guid auld Blackfriars Wynd!
Lucky to be living here in Blackfriars Wynd!
Happy and content
Amang our ain kind
Hinging aathegither here in Blackfriars Wynd!

ken, know
guddle, mess
sic, such
trauchle, struggle
thole, tolerate, suffer

For Blackfriars Wynd see
page 25.

NIGHT LIFE

From AULD REIKIE
By ROBERT FERGUSSON

Now Night, that's cunzied chief for fun,
Is wi' her usual rites begun;
Thro' ilka gate the torches blaze,
And globes send out their blinking rays.
The usefu' cadie plies in street,
To bide the profits o' his feet;
For by thir lads Auld Reikie's fock
Ken but a sample o' the stock
O' thieves that nightly wad oppress,
And make baith goods and gear the less.
Near him the lazy chairman stands,
And wats na how to turn his hands,
Till some daft birky, ranting fu'
Has matters somewhere else to do;
The chairman willing, gi'es his light
To deeds o' darkness and o' night:
    It's never sax pence for a lift
That gars thir lads wi' fu'ness rift;
For they wi' better gear are paid,
And whores and culls support their trade.
    Near some lamp-post, wi' dowy face,
Wi' heavy een, and sour grimace,
Stands she that beauty lang had kend,
Whoredom her trade, and vice her end.
But see wharenow she wuns her bread,
By that which Nature ne'er decreed;
And sings sad music to the lugs,
'Mang burachs o' damn'd whores and rogues
Whane'er we reputation loss,
Fair chastity's transparent gloss!
Redemption seenil kens the name
But a's black misery and shame.
    Frae joyous tavern, reeling drunk,
Wi' fiery phizz, and ein half sunk,
Behad the bruiser, fae to a'
That in the reek o' gardies fa':
Close by his side, a feckless race
O' macaronies shew their face,

And think they're free frae skaith or harm,
While pith befriends their leaders arm:
Yet fearfu' aften o' their maught,
They quatt the glory o' the faught
To this same warrior wha led
Thae heroes to bright honour's bed;
And aft the hack o' honour shines
In bruiser's face wi' broken lines:
Of them sad tales he tells anon,
Whan ramble and whan fighting's done;
And, like Hectorian, ne'er impairs
The brag and glory o' his sairs.
    Whan feet in dirty gutters plash,
And fock to wale their fitstaps fash;
At night the macaroni drunk,
In pools or gutters aftimes sunk:
Hegh! what a fright he now appears,
Whan he his corpse dejected rears!
Look at that head, and think if there
the pomet slaister'd up his hair!
The cheeks observe, where now cou'd shine
The scancing glories o' carmine?
Ah, legs! in vain the silk-worm there
Display'd to view her eidant care;
For stink, instead of perfumes, grow,
And clairty odours fragrant flow.
    Now some to porter, some to punch,
Some to their wife, and some their wench,
Retire, while noisy ten-hours drum
Gar's a' your trades gae dandring home.
Now mony a club, jocose and free,
Gie a' to merriment and glee;
Wi' sang and glass, they fley the pow'r
O' care that wad harrass the hour:
For wine and Bacchus still bear down
Our thrawart fortunes wildest frown:
It maks you stark, and bauld, and brave,
Ev'n whan descending to the grave.

cunzied, acknowledged	ein, eyes	skaith, hurt	slaister'd, greased
ilka, every	kend, known	maught, strength	eidant, diligent
cadie, one who runs errands	burachs, groups	faught, fight	clairty, dirty
birky, fellow	seenil, seldom	sairs, wounds	dandrin, wondering
rantin fu', cheering drunk	kens, knows	fock, folk	thrawart, perverse, hostile
culls, fools	gardies, arms	fash, trouble	
dowy, gloomy	feckless, weak		

From TO LI PO[1] IN THE DELECTABLE MOUNTAINS OF TIEN-MU[2]

In Memoriam Robert Fergusson[3] in the Blythfu Fields
Frae the Auk[4] in Auld Reekie

By SYDNEY GOODSIR SMITH

Robert Fergusson

oorie, weird, dismal
drowie haar, wet hoar-frost
mouswabs, cobwebs
airn, iron
loom-bund, fogbound
cantie, snog, cheerful, snug
howff, pub
crousie, convivial
ken, know
nocht, not
waa, wall

An ourie nicht was yesternicht,
Li Po, sir, in Auld Reekie here.
Dooms cauld it was
Cauld as the Viking hell,
Boozan doun the Royal Mile
The hinder-end o Februar
Month o fevers
    (As, Sir Precentor, ye'll mynd weill);
The drowie haar
Like icie mouswabs
Hung in the airn streets;
No monie folk abraid; and the lamps
Glauman out like loom-bund ships. . . .
At the Canongate fuit,
Lichtless and silent as a jail
The great Palace sleepit.

But in the bar
Outby across the road
By Mary's Bath-tub, aa
Was cantie, snog, and bricht,
A cheerie howff, and a crousie companie
O' philosophers and tinks - Aa
"Scholards an' gennemen, beGode!"

- A wee thing douncome i' the world maybe
But nane the waur o yon,
I'd hae ye ken.
A man's a man!
    And has, forbye,
    Belike as nocht,
    A near-in cousin
    I' the ministrie
    Or medicine, teachin,
    Or the law - ay, *law!*
    - Jungle law, o course -
    Or maybe's a collegiate
    Professor (juist)
    In some ither deeper mysterie
    - As "Real Auld Scotch"
    Or "Cute wee hoors",
    Petrol, fags, or nylons . . .
               Etcetera . . .
    Och, man, ye ken it aa!

Ay, a crousie companie, a cheerie howff
And the whiskie was liquid ingots,
Dauds o the purest gowd!
- Like Darnley's broiderit wallicoat
There hingan on the waa.

[1]*Flourit c. 750.*
[2]*Paradise.* [3]*N. 1750.*
[4]*Hoc fecit 1950.*

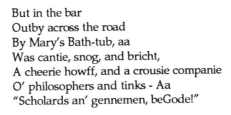

For Precentor see page 26.
For Mary's Bath-tub, see page 9.
For Darnley, see pages 8, 12 and 18-19.
For Goodsir Smith see page 35.

From HOGMANAY

By FORBES MACGREGOR

Gin like mysel ye're Embro-bred
And loe a guid-gaun ballant
In auld Scots style aboot the Mile
Whaur ye yince played as callant,
Then hae this gratis. Haun it on
When ye hae read your fill
But mind the neist to share the feast
'S as canty as yoursel
And wyce this nicht
At Christ's Kirk at the Tron.

Or I gaed up the Canogate
Last Hogmany but three
I drappit in on Coul MacFinn
To birl his barley-bree.
He stroaned the guid Glen Leevit oot
My gusty mutchkin intil,
Syne bouksome fu wi fersellin broo
I stachert yont the lintel
No blate that nicht
To Christ's Kirk at the Tron.

As I drew nigh White Horse Close-end
Guid faith, I heard a neighin;
Far doon the pend, the Deil forfend,
Oor makars' cuddies brayin:
Wud Pegasos was flichterin roun
Scairtin the chimly wa's;
Ilk makar's steed o dowf Dutch leid
To flee had little cause
Eird-fast this nicht
O' Christ's Kirk at the Tron.

Athort the gurly causey-stanes,
Like Slaver Nick's ain galleon,
Queensberry's Ha the neist I saw
That reekt o reestit hallion:
Forenent a genocidal lowe
I saw puir Scotland speetit
While eediot Bull wi' hungry gull
Drooled gantin aye and greetit
Puir-moothed this nicht
At Christ's Kirk at the Tron.

64

From CALLER OYSTERS

By ROBERT FERGUSSON

Whan big as burns the gutters rin,
Gin ye hae catcht a droukit skin,
To Luckie Middlemist's loup in
          And sit fu snug
O'er oysters and a dram o' gin,
          Or haddock lug.

When auld Saunt Giles, at aught o'clock,
Gars merchant lowns their chopies lock,
There we adjourn wi' hearty fock
          To birle our bodles,
And get wharewi' to crack our joke,
          And clear our noddles.

loe, love
callant, youth
canty, cheerful
mutchkin, about a pint
bouksome, of large size
fersellin, energising
stachert, staggered
blate, timid, backward
pend, covered way
forfend, forbid
wud, mad
flichterin, fluttering
scairtin, scratching
leid, language
eird-fast, earthbound
athort, across
gurly causie stanes, rough street
  stones
neist, nearest
reekt o reestit hallion, smelled of
  smoked vulgar woman
lowe, flame
gantin, yawning, stuttering
droukit, drenched
loup, leap
aught, eight
gars, makes
chopies, shops
birle, spend freely
bodles, two pennies Scots
noddles, heads

For Tron Kirk see page 13.
White Horse Close in the
Canongate was the site in the
seventeenth century of White
Horse Inn which was said to be
named after a white palfrey
ridden by Mary Queen of Scots,
see page 9.
Queensberry Ha was owned by
the Duke of Queensberry; the 2nd
Duke was influential in making
possible the Treaty of Union
of 1707.
For Luckie Middlemist's
see page 26.

FROM AULD REIKIE

By ROBERT FERGUSSON

But chief, O Cape! we crave thy aid,
To get our cares and poortith laid:
Sincerity, and genius true,
Of Knights have ever been the due:
Mirth, music, porter deepest dy'd,
Are never here to worth deny'd:
And health, o' happiness the queen,
Blinks bonny, wi' her smile serene.

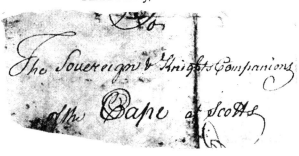

poortith, poverty
rickle o' banes, skin and bones
syne, then
dowie, weak
ocht, anything
kir, cheerful
lauchin, laughing
loupit, jumped
skites, flies off
heich skeich, high spirited
tashed, battered
muckle, much
creeshy, fat
kythed, emerged
auld carline, old woman

For MacDiarmid see page 19 and 20.
For Cape Club see pages 26 - 7.

OLD WIFE IN HIGH SPIRITS
In an Edinburgh Pub

By HUGH MACDIARMID

An auld wumman cam' in, a mere rickle o' banes, in a faded black dress
And a bonnet wi' beads o' jet rattlin' on it;
A puir-lookin' cratur, you'd think she could hardly ha'e had less
Life left in her and still lived, but dagonit!

He gied her a stiff whisky - she was nervous as a troot
And could haurdly haud the tumbler, puir cratur;
Syne he gied her anither, joked wi' her, and anither, and syne
Wild as the whisky up cam' her nature.

The rod that struck water frae the rock in the desert
Was naething to the life that sprang oot o' her;
The dowie auld soul was twinklin' and fizzin' wi fire;
You never saw ocht sae souple and kir.

Like a sackful o' monkeys she was, and her lauchin'
Loupit up whiles to incredible heights;
Wi' ane owre the eight her temper changed and her tongue
Flew juist as the forkt lichtnin' skites.

The heich skeich auld cat was fair in her element;
Wanton as a whirlwind, and shairly better that way
Than a' crippen thegither wi' laneliness and cauld
Like a foretaste o' the graveyaird clay.

Some folk naw doot'll condemn gie'in' a guid spree
To the puir dune body and raither she endit her days
Like some auld tashed copy o' the Bible yin sees
On a street book-barrow's tipenny trays,

A' I ken is weel-fed and weel-put-on though they be
Ninety per cent o' respectable folk never hae
As muckle life in their creeshy carcases frae beginnin' to end
As kythed in that wild auld carline that day!

WILLIE BREW'D A PECK O' MAUT

By ROBERT BURNS

Chorus

O Willie brew'd a peck o' maut,
  And Rob and Allan cam to see;
Three blyther hearts, that lee lang night,
  Ye wad na found in Christendie.

Chorus

We are na fou, we're nae that fu,
  But just a drappie in our e'e;
The cock may craw, the day may daw,
  And ay we'll taste the barley bree.

Here are we met, three merry boys,
  Three merry boys I trow are we;
And mony a night we've merry been,
  And mony mae we hope to be!

It is the moon, I ken her horn,
  That's blinkin in the lift sae hie;
She shines sae bright to wyle us hame,
  But by my sooth she'll wait a wee!

Wha first shall rise to gang awa,
  A cuckold, coward loun is he!
Wha first beside his chair shall fa'
  He is the king amang us three!

maut, malt
lee lang, live long
fou, drunk
drappie, drop
e'e, eye
bree, brew
mony mae, mony more
lift, sky
wyle, entice
wee, bit
loun, fellow
fa', fall

For details of Willie Nicol see
page 19 and epitaph on page 76.
Allan was Allan Masterton, like
Nicol a High School teacher.

LOVE

Courtship

Robert Burns

Clarinda

A RONDEL OF LUVE

By ALEXANDER SCOTT

Lo, quhat it is to lufe!
Lerne, ye that list to prufe,
be me, I say, that no ways may
the grund of grief remufe,
bot still decay both nycht and day.
Lo, quhat it is to lufe!

Lufe is ane fervent fire
kendillit without desire,
schort plesour, lang displesour.
Repentence is the hire,
ane pure tressour without mesour.
Lufe is ane fervent fire.

To lufe and to be wyis,
to rege with gud advyis,
now thus, now than, so gois the game:
incertane is the dyis.
Thair is no man, I say, that can
both lufe and to be wyis.

Fle alwayis frome the snair.
Lerne at me to be ware.
It is ane pane and dowbill trane
of endles wo and cair.
For to refrane that denger plane
fle alwayis frome the snair.

kendillit, kindled
without desire, unsolicited,
unsought
bire, wage, reward
pure, poor
advyis, deliberation
dyis, dice

Alexander Scott (c.1515-c.1583)
see page 8.

From UNDER THE EILDON TREE

By SYDNEY GOODSIR SMITH

The lums o' the reikan toun
Spreid aa ablow, and round
As far as ye could look
The yalla squares o' winnocks
Lit ilkane by a nakit yalla sterne
Blenkan, aff, syne on again,
Out and in and out again,
As the thrang mercat throve,
    The haill toun at it
Aa the lichts pip-poppan
    In and out and in again
        I' the buts and bens
            And single ends,
                The banks and braes
O' the toueran cliffs o' lands,
Haill tenements, wards and burghs, counties,
    Regalities and jurisdictiouns,
        Continents and empires
            Gien ower entire
Til the joukerie-poukerie!
Hech, sirs, whatna feck of fockerie!
Shades o' Knox, the hochmagandie!
    My bonie Edinburrie
        Auld Skulduggerie!
Flat on her back sevin nichts o' the week,
Earnan her breid wi' her hurdies' sweit.

- And Dian's siller chastitie
Muved owre the reikan lums,
Biggan a ferlie toun of jet and ivorie
That was but blackened stane,
Whar Bothwell rade and Huntly
And fair Montrose and aa the lave
Wi silken leddies doun til the grave.
    - The hoofs strak siller on the causie!
        And I myself in cramasie!

lums, chimneys
reikan, smoking
winnocks, windows
sterne, star
syne, then
thrang, busy
buts and bens, two-roomed
    houses
single-ends, one-roomed
    flats
joukerie-poukerie, roguery
hochmagandie, fornication
hurdies, buttocks
siller, siller
ferlie, marvel
aa, all
lave, rest
cause, street
cramasie, crimson silk
For Sydney Goodsir Smith
see page 35.
For John Knox see page 12.
For Bothwell see page 8.
For Montrose see page 16.

OLD COUPLE IN A BAR

By NORMAN MACCAIG

They sit without speaking, looking straight ahead.
They've said it all before, they've seen it all before.
They're content.

They sit without moving: Ozymandias and Sphinx.

He says something! - and she answers, smiling,
and taps him flirtatiously on the arm:
Daphnis and Chloe: with Edinburgh accents.

Illustration from
Walter Perrie's book
By Moon and Sun

FLEURS-DE-LYS

By ALEXANDER HUTCHISON

Sullen girls like lilies,
see them: sulkily listening
to music. Does duty put that
look upon them of languid
disinterest, lids downcast.
It may be duty (sitting where
they do), but beauty marks
them: pale and perfect, lily
flowers. Round and above them,
a cappella, voices winding.
Sullen, lovely, eyes averted,
devotees of a pure disdain.

For Fleurs-de-lys see page 13.

From BY MOON AND SUN

By WALTER PERRIE

City, city
        so much loved
                        precarious our balance is
between Schiehallion
                and the damned.

Sweet prince, by candle light
                        let's love
unless the street lamp should betray
                        too harshly
tears for sundering
        for seed and shooting stars
                        all dimmed
                        diminished
our inheritance to this
                one bar, one star
                two seedling tears
of muddy waters
        fiery airs.

AE FOND KISS
Tune, Rory Dall's port

By ROBERT BURNS

Slow and tender

ROBERT BURNS

Ae fond kiss, and then we sever;
Ae fareweel, and then for ever!
Deep in heart-wrung tears I'll pledge thee,
Warring sighs and groans I'll wage thee. -

Who shall say that Fortune grieves him,
While the star of hope she leaves him:
Me, nae chearful twinkle lights me;
Dark despair around benights me. -

I'll ne'er blame my partial fancy,
Naething could resist my Nancy;
But to see her, was to love her;
Love but her, and love for ever. -

Had we never lov'd sae kindly,
Had we never lov'd sae blindly!
Never met - or never parted,
We had ne'er been broken-hearted. -

Fare-thee-weel, thou first and fairest!
Fare-thee-weel, thou best and dearest!
Thine be ilka joy and treasure,
Peace, Enjoyment, Love and Pleasure! -

Ae fond kiss, and then we sever!
Ae fareweel, Alas, for ever!
Deep in heart-wrung tears I'll pledge thee,
Warring sighs and groans I'll wage thee. -

Nancy is Mrs McLehose,
"Clarinda".

For Clarinda see pages 9, 19, 20
and 31.

TWO SHADOW^S IN CONVERSATION

DuKe
and
Duche∫s

LORD MONBODDO

From TO THE MERCHANTIS OF EDINBURGH

By WILLIAM DUNBAR

Quhy will ye, merchantis of renoun,
Lat Edinburgh, your nobill toun,
For laik of reformatioun
The commone proffeitt tyine and fame?
   Think ye not schame,
That onie uther regioun
Sall with dishonour hurt your name!

May nane pas throw your principall gaittis
For stink of haddockis and of scattis
For cryis of carlingis and debaittis,
For fensum flyttingis of defame:
   Think ye not schame,
Befoir strangeris of all estaittis
That sic dishonour hurt your name!

Your stinkand Style, that standis dirk,
Haldis the lycht fra your parroche kirk;
Your foirstairis makis your housis mirk,
Lyk na cuntray bot heir at hame:
   Think ye not schame,
Sa litill polesie to wirk
In hurt and sklander of your name!

At your hie Croce, quhar gold and silk
Sould be, thair is bot crudis and milk:
And at your Trone bot cokill and wilk,
Panshes, pudingis of Jok and Jame:
   Think ye not schame,
Sen as the world sayis that ilk
In hurt and sclander of your name!

Your commone menstrallis hes no tone
Bot 'Now the day dawis,' and 'Into Joun';
Cunningar men man serve Sanct Cloun,
And nevir to uther craftis clame;
   Think ye not schame,
To hald sic mowaris on the moyne,
In hurt and sclander of your name!

Tailyouris, soutteris, and craftis vyll,
The fairest of your streitis dois fyll;
And merchandis at the Stinkand Styll
Ar hamperit in ane hony came:
   Think ye not schame,
That ye have nether witt nor wyll
To win yourselff ane bettir name!

Your burgh of beggeris is ane nest,
To schout thai swentyouris will not rest;
All honest folk they do molest,
Sa piteuslie thai cry and rame:
   Think ye not schame,
That for the poore hes nothing drest,
In hurt and sclander of your name!

Your proffeit daylie dois incres,
Your godlie workis les and les;
Through streittis nane may mak progres
For cry of cruikit, blind, and lame:
   Think ye not shame,
That ye sic substance dois posses,
And will nocht win ane bettir name!

tyine, lose
carlingis, old women
fensum flyttingis, offensive denunciations
stinkand Style, passageway between
  (Luckenbooths), tenements of shops
parroche kirk, St Giles' Church
pansches, tripe

tone, tune
mowaris, jokers
soutteris, shoemakers
came, comb
swentyouris, rogues
rame, clamour
nocht, nothing

For Dunbar see pages 7-8, 9,
10 and 27.
For Luckenbooths see
pages 27-8.
For St Giles see pages 14-16.

From KYND KITTOCK'S LAND

By SYDNEY GOODSIR SMITH

I

This rortie wretched city
Sair come doun frae its auld hiechts
- The hauf o't smug, complacent,
Lost til all pride of race or spirit,
The tither wild and rouch as ever
In its secret hairt
But lost alsweill, the smeddum tane,
The man o' independent mind has cap in hand the day
- Sits on its craggy spine
And drees the wind and rain
That nourished all its genius
- Weary wi centuries
This empty capital snorts like a great beast
Caged in its sleep, dreaming of freedom
But with nae belief,
Indulging an auld ritual
Whase meaning's been forgot owre lang,
A mere habit of words - when the drink's in -
And signifying naething.

This rortie wretched city
Built on history
Built of history
Born of feud and enmity
Suckled on bluid and treachery
Its lullabies the clash of steel
And shouted slogan, sits here in her lichtit cage,
A beast wi the soul o' an auld runkled whure,
Telling her billies o' her granderie in auld lang syne
- Oh ay, it was grand and glorious,
Splendant wi banners and nobilitie
- Nae greater granderie were was
Than was kent by thae grey stanes
But nou - juist memories for towrists - Ha!

II

Gang doun the hill. Ye get mair noble
As ye gang, or less, past Deacon Brodie
Elevated thrice for his thieveries,
Twice on pubs and aince
For aa time on his ain patent gibbet -
A kin' o' ghoulish joke -
Ach, Aiberdeen, you never had the like o' yon;
Auld Reekie wins at that, at least!

But at the fute o' the Mile ye're juist
As hiech as ye can get wi the jessie Darnley's
Silken waistcoat on the wall
And Mary's Bathtub gey nearhaundy
And gey cauld, ye'd think.
       A queerlike canyon is the Canongate,
That murmurs yet wi the names
O' lang deid bards - alack,
Auld Rabbie's Bar is gane
But Honest Allan's there
And the ghaist o' the Electric Shepherd
(As they cry him)
Still hauds up his boozie snoot for nourishment:
Puir Fergusson's forgot, eheu! Eheu!

For Deacon Brodie see page 26.
For Darnley see pages 8, 12 and 18-19.
For Mary's Bathtub see page 9,
and Lewis Spence's poem on page 46.
Honest Allan is Ramsay see pages 9, 13,
22, 27, and 34-5.
The Electric Shepherd is James Hogg
the Ettrick Shepherd.
For Kynd Kittock see page 35.

* * *

auld heichts, old heights	billies, fellows
rouch, rough	auld lang syne, times past
smeddum, gumption	kent, known
drees, endures	heich, high
auld runkled, old wrinkled	

From THE GHAISTS: A KIRK-YARD ECLOGUE

By ROBERT FERGUSSON

Watson

Cauld blaws the nippin north wi' angry sough,
And showers his hailstanes frae the Castle Cleugh
O'er the Greyfriars, whare, at mirkest hour,
Bogles and spectres wont to tak their tour,
Harlin' the pows and shanks to hidden cairns,
Amang the hamlocks wild, and sun-burnt fearns,
But nane the night save you and I hae come
Frae the dern mansions of the midnight tomb.
Now whan the dawning's near, whan cock maun craw,
And wi' his angry bougil gar's withdraw,
Ayont the kirk we'll stap, and there tak bield,
While the black hours our nightly freedom yield.

Watson

Sure Major Weir, or some sic warlock wight,
Has flung beguilin' glamer o'er your sight;
Or else some kittle cantrup thrown, I ween,
Has bound in mirlygoes my ain twa ein,
If ever aught frae sense cou'd be believ'd
(And seenil hae my senses been deceiv'd),
This moment, o'er the tap of Adam's tomb,
Fu' easy can I see your chiefest dome:
Nae corbie fleein' there, nor croupin' craws,
Seem to forspeak the ruin of thy haws,
But a' your tow'rs in wonted order stand,
Steeve as the rocks that hem our native land.

Herriot

I'm weel content; but binna cassen down,
Nor trow the cock will ca' ye hame o'er soon,
For tho' the eastern lift betakens day,
Changing her rokelay black for mantle grey,
Nae weirlike bird our knell of parting rings,
Nor sheds the caller moisture frae his wings.
Nature has chang'd her course; the birds o' day
Dosin' in silence on the bending spray,
While owlets round the craigs at noon-tide flee,
And bludey bawks sit singand on the tree.
Ah, Caledon! the land I yence held dear,
Sair mane mak I for thy destruction near;
And thou, Edina! anes my dear abode,
Whan royal Jamie sway'd the sovereign rod,
In thae blest days, weel did I think bestow'd,
To blaw thy poortith by wi' heaps o' gowd;
To mak thee sonsy seem wi' mony a gift,
And gar thy stately turrets speel the lift:
In vain did Danish Jones, wi' gimcrack pains,
In Gothic sculpture fret the pliant stanes:
In vain did he affix my statue here,
Brawly to busk wi' flow'rs ilk coming year;
My tow'rs are sunk, my lands are barren now,
My fame, my honour, like my flow'rs maun dow.

mirkest, darkest
sough, breath
Cleugh, rock
harlin, dragging
pows, heads
dern, secret, hidden
gars, makes
ayont, beyond
bield, shelter
binna, be not
cassen, cast
rokelay, mantle
caller, cool
bawks, bats
poortith, poverty
gowd, gold
sonsy, fortunate
gar, make
speel, climb
lift, sky
gimcrack, tawdry, fantastic
busk, dress, deck
ilk, every
maun dow, must wither
sic warlock wight, such warlock fellow
glamer, bewitchment
kittle cantrup, mysterious charm
mirlygoes, illusions
ein, eyes
aught, anything
seenil, seldom
corbie, raven
steeve, firm

For Heriot see pages 20, 22, 26 and 27.
For Watson see page 22.
For Greyfriars Kirkyard see page 22.
Danish Jones is Inigo Jones
who was popularly thought to have
designed Heriot's Hospital.
For Major Weir see page 21.

The reason for the complaints of the
ghaists was that in 1773 the charities such as
Heriot and Watson had founded were seen as
being threatened with regard to income
by the Mortmain Bill, which was intended to
empower trustees to invest their funds in
government securities, based in London.

George Heriot

EDINBURGH WALKABOUT

By DUNCAN GLEN

i

I walk the Auld Toon.

It's a close o high-risin stane. I crane roond
turning stairwey and see there Boswell and Hume. I gie
a thocht to mony ither residents.
Folk wi smeddum, folk withoot name, lang gane.

A froon. The Auld Toon. The medieval hings in the air.
And there, still, the smell, the guff, rancid,
sweet-soor. Soon there'll be modernisation,
this turnpike lose its grime, if no its smell,

be o oor time,
                    — aw, surface.

ii

I'm revisitin Edinburgh Castle.

A clear cauld day. I'll staun alane as years afore
in St Margaret's bare stane chapel. No that I hae
Christian faith that I can tell. I walk
to whaur I thocht it stood. I canna find it!

Will I ask that kiltit sodger? I mind the chapel on heich
position. Ither sodgers merch by. But I'll no ask.
And then, there it is. Should I gie it a miss? I walk
in. There's a rope wi attendant seatit ahint

— and the waws are pentit white
                              for guid or ill.

thocht, thought
smeddum, gumption
guff, a bad smell
turnpike, turning stair
aw, all
heich, high
pentit, painted
rouch, rough

For the courts and Boswell
and Hume see pages 32 and 34.
For St Margaret's Chapel see
page 7.
For Greyfriars Bobby see
page 22.

iii

I'm to the Gallery of Modern Art.

I staun afore "Reclinin Figure" by Henry Moore.
I think o Michelangelo. The greatest o airtists
hae nae thocht to what the rouch stane
in its superfluous shell disnae include.

To brak the marble spell, that is aw
the haund that sers the brain can dae. And this
perhaps the maist famous piece o sculpture
in Scotland

till you think o
                    —Greyfriars Bobby.

75

From TO WILLIAM CREECH

By ROBERT BURNS

Auld chuckie Reekie's sair distrest,
Down droops her ance weel-burnish'd crest,
Nae joy her bonie buskit nest
     Can yield ava;
Her darling bird that she loes best,
     Willie's awa. -

O Willie was a witty wight,
And had o' things an unco slight;
Auld Reekie ay he keepit tight,
     And trig and braw:
But now they'll busk her like a fright,
     Willie's awa. -

The stiffest o' them a' he bow'd,
The bauldest o' them a' he cow'd,
They durst nae mair than he allow'd,
     That was a law:
We've lost a birkie weel worth gowd,
     Willie's awa. -

Now gawkies, tawpies, gowks and fools,
Frae colleges and boarding-schools,
May sprout like simmer puddock-stools
     In glen or shaw;
He wha could brush them down to mools
     Willie's awa. -

The brethren o' the commerce-chaumer
May mourn their loss wi' doolfu' clamour;
He was a dictionar and grammar
     Amang them a':
I fear they'll now mak mony a stammer,
     Willie's awa. -

Nae mair we see his levée door
Philosophers and Poets pour,
And toothy Critics by the score
     In bloody raw;
The Adjutant of a' the core
     Willie's awa. -

EPITAPH FOR WILLIAM NICOL

By ROBERT BURNS

Ye maggots, feed on Willie's brains,
    For few sic feasts ye've gotten;
An' fix your claws into his heart,
    For fient a bit o't 's rotten.

William Creech

chuckie, mother-hen
ane, once
buskit, well-furnished, dressed up
loes, loves
wight, fellow
unco, odd
trig, neet
busk, dress up
birkie, spry fellow
gowd, gold
gawkies, fools
tawpies, senseless girls
gowks, dolts
simmer puddock-stools, summer
  toadstools
shaw, smallwood in a hollow
  lacep
mools, graves, grave clods
commerce-chaumer, chamber of
  commerce
doolful, sorrowful
stammer, stumble

For Creech see pages 27 and 30.
For Burns in Edinburgh see
pages 19-20 and 30-2.
For Nicol see page 19.

TWO CHARACTER SKETCHES

By ROBERT BURNS

1
WILLIAM CREECH

A little, upright, pert, tart, tripping wight,
And still his precious Self his dear delight;
Who loves his own smart shadow in the streets
Better then e'er the fairest fair he meets.
Much specious lore, but little understood,
Fineering oft outshines the solid wood:
A man of fashion too, he made his tour,
Learn'd vive la bagatelle et vive l'amour;
So travell'd monkies their grimace improve,
Polish their grin, nay sigh for ladies' love:
His meddling Vanity, a busy fiend,
Still making work his Selfish-craft must mend -

2
WILLIAM SMELLIE

     Crochallan came;
The old cock'd hat, the brown surtout the same;
His grisly beard just bristling in its might,
'Twas four long nights and days from shaving-night;
His uncomb'd, hoary locks, wild-staring, thatch'd,
A head for thought profound and clear unmatch'd:
Yet, tho' his caustic wit was biting rude,
His heart was warm, benevolent and good.

Wiliam Smellie

SELF PORTRAIT

By ALLAN RAMSAY

Imprimis then, for tallness I
Am five foot and four inches high:
A black-a-vic'd snod dapper fallow,
Nor lean, nor overlaid wi' tallow.
With phiz of a Morocco cut,
Resembling a late man of wit,
Auld-gabbet *Spec,* wha was sae cunning
To be a dummie ten years running.

THE SEAT O' INSPIRATION

By DOUGLAS FRASER

(Amang the Burns relics at Lady Stair's
Hoose are twa stules used by the Poet when
correctin priefs at the printer's)

I rubbed my dowp on Rabbie's stule
When naebody was by,
Ae day at Lady Stair's braw Hoose;
Forgie me gin I craw owre croose
But, fegs, I hae a graun excuse -
Ye'll ken the reason why.

Rab had mair genius in his dowp,
I'd be prepared to bet,
Than a' the wits o' ilka schule
Could muster in a common pule.
I rubbed my dowp on Rabbie's stule -
I'll be a poet yet!

doup, backside
ae, one
gin, if
ilka, every

For Smellie see page 26.
For Allan Ramsay see pages 9,
13, 22, 27and 34-5.
What I have titled "Self Portrait"
is from "An Epistle to Mr James
Arbuckle of Belfast".
For Burns's stool see page 26.

O. & B.

By JOHN W. OLIVER

Far in the depths of Tweeddale Court,
    Hard by the Royal Mile,
Within an ancient mansion
    Built in stately Georgian style,
All day there sit two wise old blokes,
    On solemn tasks employed.
The one is Mr Oliver;
    The t'other's Mr Boyd.

They sit beside a table
    That is heaped with MSS,
And they wonder how the dickens
    They can fit them for the press;
And everyone they look at
    Seems to make them more annoyed;
For a grim old chap is Oliver,
    But grimmer still is Boyd.

I sent them late a book of verse
    In brightest comic style:
They looked at it with sour distaste
    And did not deign to smile:
They scanned my brightest efforts,
    And they found them null and void:
"I'm not amused," said Oliver:
    "They bore me stiff," said Boyd.

I tried them with a novel
    That was modern as could be,
And full of all the clichés
    From the new Psychologee;
It was packed with strange and startling things
    I'd culled from Dr Freud;
But - "It's rather dull," said Oliver;
    "It's bunkum!" thundered Boyd.

So they damn your brightest efforts,
    And they don't make no mistake,
Then toddle quietly homeward,
    To peruse a "Sexton Blake";
And, as they turn its pages o'er
    With pleasure unalloyed,
"This is the stuff," says Oliver;
    "It's champion," says Boyd.

TWEEDDALE COURT

(Fir the Scottish Poetry Library
and aa wha yuise it)

By TOM HUBBARD

Whan at the boddom o this auncient stracht
We stude afore the yett, an keekit throu,
We kent thon gaitherin wis nae fir us.
Upon retour, we thocht ti sclim the hicht
Ti see the nation spreid oot glorious -
A thrang o sodgers kept us fae the view.
Wis there nae walcome in this dour auld toun
For ocht but gowd an fecht? We lear the fate
o yin wha tint thaim aa, an cam this gate -
Montrose, a makar - ti be dingit doun . . .
But suddent, mid o the Mile, we fin this close
o murtherous repute, whaur we feel free,
An makars win throu sturt fir fowk lik us
Wha hinna been sae near ti haurmonie.

boddom, bottom
auncient stracht, old street
yett, gate
retour, return
sclim the hicht, climb the height
thrang o sodgers, busy crowd of
    soldiers
ocht but gowd an fecht, aught but
    gold and fight
tint, lost
dingit, smashed, fall
sturt, conflict
hinna, have not.

For Tweeddale Court see page 12.
For Oliver & Boyd see page 12.
For Tom Hubbard see page 12.
For Montrose see page 16.

TO THE TRON-KIRK BELL

By ROBERT FERGUSSON

Wanwordy, crazy, dinsome thing,
As e'er was fram'd to jow or ring,
What gar'd them sic in steeple hing
       They ken themsel',
But weel wat I they coudna bring
       War sounds frae hell.

What de'il are ye? that I shud ban,
Your neither kin to pat nor pan;
Not uly pig, nor master-cann,
       But weel may gie
Mair pleasure to the ear o' man
       Than stroak o' thee.

Fleece merchants may look bald, I trow,
Sin a' Auld Reikie's childer now
Maun stap their lugs wi' teats o' woo,
       Thy sound to bang,
And keep it frae gawn thro' and thro'
       Wi' jarrin' twang.

Your noisy tongue, there's nae abideint,
Like scaulding wifes, there is nae guideint;
Whan I'm 'bout ony bus'ness eident,
       It's sair to thole;
To deave me, than, ye tak' a pride in't
       Wi' senseless knoll.

O! war I provost o' the town,
I swear by a' the pow'rs aboon,
I'd bring ye wi' a reesle down;
       Nor shud you think
(Sae sair I'd crack and clour your crown)
       Again to clink.

For whan I've toom'd the muckle cap,
An' fain wud fa' owr in a nap,
Troth I cud doze as sound's a tap,
       Wer't na for thee,
That gies the tither weary chap
       To waukin me.

I dreamt ae night I saw Auld Nick;
Quo he, "this bell o' mine's a trick,
A wylie piece o' politic,
       A cunnin snare
To trap fock in a cloven stick,
       'Ere they're aware.

As lang's my dautit bell hings there,
A' body at the kirk will skair;
Quo they, 'gif he that preaches there
       Like it can wound,
We douna care a single hair
       For joyfu' sound.'"

If magistrates wi' me wud 'gree,
For ay tongue-tackit shud you be,
Nor fleg wi' antimelody
       Sic honest fock,
Whase lugs were never made to dree
       Thy doolfu' shock.

But far frae thee the bailies dwell,
Or they wud scunner at your knell,
Gie the foul thief his riven bell,
       And than, I trow,
The by-word hads, "the de'il himsel'
       Has got his due".

wanwordy, worthless
jow, toll
gar'd, caused
sic, such
weel wat, well know
war, worse
de'il, devil
pat, pot
pig, jar
master-can, vessel for
  holding urine
trow, believe
childer, children
maun stap, must fill
wo, wool
eident, diligent
sair to thole, difficult to
  endure
deave, stun the ears with
  noise
war, were
reesle, clatter
clour, batter
toom'd, emptied
muckle, large
fain, gladly
chap, strike
Auld Nick, the devil
dautit, doted
skair, scare
fleg, frighten
dree, suffer
doolfu, sorrowful
scunner, be sickened
de'il, devil

For Tron-kirk bell see page 13.

TWA FESTIVAL SKETCHES

By ROBERT GARIOCH

I

I wes passing a convertit kirk -
        Whit's that ye say?
A convertit kirk, plenty o thaim about;
the kirks yuistae convert the sinners,
bit nou the sinners convert the kirks.
Weill oniewey, here wes this convertit kirk
wi bills stuck owre the front
and folk queuin up to git in
to hear the Po-etic Gems
o William McGonagall.
On the pavement outside
there was a richt rammie gaun on,
folk millin about, ken?
And in the middle o this rammie
wes a man that wes gittin   Moved On -
        Whit fir? -
He'd been sellin   broadsheets
o poems, Gode help him!
o his ain composition.

II

At the Tattoo
they hae twa-three collapsible cot-houssis.
We behold a typical Hieland Scena:
a typical blacksmith dingan on his stiddie,
and a typical drouth boozan at the nappie -
the usquebaugh, I should say -
        et cetera.
Alang comes the Duchess o Gordon on horseback.
She wants sodgers
and the Hielands are fou of Hielandmen.
She gies til each recruit a blue-bluidit kiss.
Nou the boozan has ceased.
The smiddie fire is out.
The Duchess o Gordon has gien them
the Kiss o Daith.

HEROES

By NORMAN MACCAIG

The heroes of legend
and the heroes of history
met, by looking
in a mirror.

And the heroes of legend
capered with joy,
crying,
"We're real, we're real!"

And the heroes of history
wept with rage
and wanted
to smash the mirror.

But that would mean they'd cease
to exist. So they dried their eyes
and assumed once more
their insufferable poses.

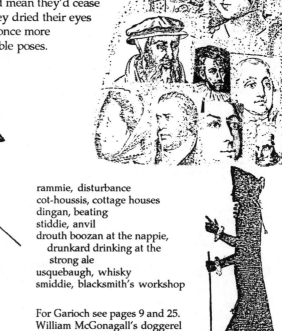

rammie, disturbance
cot-houssis, cottage houses
dingan, beating
stiddie, anvil
drouth boozan at the nappie,
    drunkard drinking at the
    strong ale
usquebaugh, whisky
smiddie, blacksmith's workshop

For Garioch see pages 9 and 25.
William McGonagall's doggerel
is published under the title *Poetic
Gems*.
The Duchess of Gordon kissed
each recruit.

FRAE EDINBURGH'S HIGH STREET

By DUNCAN GLEN

This High street, this Royal Mile nearly
a reserve for tourists. There's
mony a safari frae Ramsay Lane to Warld's End
Close. Here anely hauf-wey
to the bitter end whaur facts are chiels
you winna ding and the unicorn
foals the fiddler.
        Here at Tron Kirk
that crazy, dinsome bell struck dumb. I stop
ootside John Knox's hoose. It looks safe,
quite tame. I see Titian's "Diana and Actaeon"
fleeing frae this hoose's lums.
        The sun keeks
owre Arthur's Seat. I staun still
by St Giles richt in the middle o this
traffic frantic street. Here see Wullie Creech's
shop and Robert Burns staunin, bein 1786,
ootside it. At this very spot and lookin
doon the tunnel o the street to glisk
o the Forth at its end. And thae
whunstane hairts carried still aneath fat
wallets. It's time I was across
the Meadows hame. The deil's cam
fiddling through the toon and Robert Burns
is awa as Exciseman.
        On me the thocht
o the lang, lang years o shot kail
flooerin owre aw Scotland. A young woman
shouts across the street, "I need food,
I'm hungry!". Dunbar for sure they've
flung owre Castle Rock. Aye the stink
o haddies and skate. There's a smert group
o kiltit sodgers walk paist. But see
an antrin thing. Aw the windaes lichtit up
yet but 1 p.m. A sicht o the infinite
and this land in that perspective. It's 1926,
a drunk man faur gane, high on rouch
auld leid. A raucle tongue, a singin voice
upliftit, lowpin, breengin in on
the unkent. There's Wellum Wallace lowpin
frae *his* niche afore the Castle. And William
Dunbar sclimin, haund owre haund
up Castle Rock. And James VI ridin north

no to be seen for stour? Will Marc Chagall jine
us, and Bella, and his violinist? We'll
sit atap the lums o this auld toon
and fiddle awa the nicht joyfully into
the morrow and themorrow.
        For the noo
I'll be to the Jolly Judge. It's ticht foo, but
sit aw my lane. On the waw aside me engravin
o Duncan Gray. Ha, ha,
the wooin o't. "What may the fruit be yet?"
And the answerin voice, "I dinna ken-
Eve's was Cain!" On the Meadows the gean
blossom has fawen. The Spring cams late
here in the north, but aye hope o less-bitter
fruit I repeat to mysel. A man gaein oot
the door says, "Aye, aye feart o oorsels!"
At a table in the faur corner a lass is
talkin o a luver, "Nae finesse!" Twa Americans are
lookin at a pentin on the waw abune the fireplace
readin key to wha is present. It's Robert Burns
giein a readin doon the road
in the Duchess o Gordon's braw salon,
bein January 1787. Hear the beatin o whunstane
hairts. Wullie Creech looks sair
at his complacent ease. A man at the baur says,
"I amna tired sae muckle as
deid done". Aye leid! Aye a flag, fadit
but raised, moves like the thunnerstorm
agin the saftnin wund. A man doonby says, slawly
"It's faur oot the wey, but gey
haundy".

antrin, strange, unusual	not to be seen for stour,
rouch auld leid, rough old	moving fast
language	dinna ken, do not know
raucle, strong	gean, cherry
lowpin, leaping	muckle as deid done,
breengin, moving impetuously	much as tired
sclimin, climbing	

For William Dunbar see pages 7-8.
For Burns in Edinburgh see pages 19, 20 and 30-2.
For A Drunk Man Looks at the Thistle see page 19.
For the Jolly Judge pub see page 32.
For Burns and the Duchess of Gordon see page 31.
For Wullie Creech see pages 27 and 30.

WINTER SUNRISE
IN EDINBURGH

By TESSA RANSFORD

The huge pale sun behind the Braid Hills
rising
glints on the city in wands of slanting light;

The threadbare half-moon hangs above
Corstorphine
where winter branches stretch and silhouette;

With sunrise in her hair the girl Queen
Mary
rode to dying Darnley out at Kirk O' Field;

On such a frosty forenoon Cockburn left
the lawcourts,
experienced the New Town, memorised the Old;

Singing a cold cadence Fergusson
the poet
shivered down the Canongate with rhythm in his feet;

And citizens of Edinburgh on this very
morning
set to partners, join hands and skip down the street.

EDINBURGH AUTUMN

By DUNCAN GLEN

It is September. There is a haar
drifting in frae the Forth
gien an air o mystery.
A cauldness in the air owre soon.

The soonds heard blurred.
It is haurd to tell from whaur
they cam. But the mist will clear
if a bit aye in the air

takin us into the beautiful
irony o autumn.

ANNALS OF
ENLIGHTENMENT

By ALEXANDER HUTCHISON

Hume passes
into the absolute,
brace-girdled, without
concern.

James,
laird of Auchinleck,
as this transpires, lays
boisterous breath along
his doxy's shoulder,

elevates the skirt,
and takes her on the dust
of a stonemason's table,
some way below
the Castle hill.

.

In or out
of armour, which
would you rather -

cool release
of the *bon philosphe*,
or Boswell's perturbation?

Much to be endured,
and little to be enjoyed?

or what mix in between?

.

At ten, a drum
for clart and creesh
on close and vennel.

The wind
in a shift lifts
leaves along old
Calton wall.

doxy's, wench's
clart and creesh,
    dirt and grease
vennel, alley

For Darnley and Kirk
o' Field see pages 18-19.
James Boswell, was laird
of Auchinleck.
For Hume and Boswell.
see page 32.
A drum was beaten at
ten p.m. when
the rubbish was
thrown onto the street,
Gardyloo, see page 27.
Old Calton Hill cemetery is
where Hume is buried.

THE CITY WE LIVE IN

By TESSA RANSFORD

You are on my skyline
as high as eye is lifted
nothing is beyond you.

I approach and
come up against
walls
your rock defences.

You bridge my extremes
lead over, across
between one level and another.

I pass within the shadow
of your arches
and walk the colonnade.

Crescent and high terrace
would not entice me but
for sudden vista:

statue, campanile,
pearl of sea, jade of hill
well-proportioned temple.

More than these
I try the narrow steps
tunnelled wynds, wrought-iron gates

that lead me where
an inner court
holds itself secluded.

NOVEMBER NIGHT,
EDINBURGH

By NORMAN MACCAIG

The night tinkles like ice in glasses.
Leaves are glued to the pavement with frost.
The brown air fumes at the shop windows,
Tries the doors, and sidles past.

I gulp down winter raw. The heady
Darkness swirls with tenements.
In a brown fuzz of cottonwool
Lamps fade up crags, die into pits.

Frost in my lungs is harsh as leaves
Scraped up on paths. - I look up, there,
A high roof sails, at the mast-head
Fluttering a gray and ragged star.

The world's a bear shrugged in his den.
It's snug and close in the snoring night.
And outside like chrysanthemums
The fog unfolds its bitter scent.

From AULD REIKIE

By ROBERT FERGUSSON

Reikie, farewell! I ne'er cou'd part
Wi' thee but wi' a dowy heart;
Aft frae the Fifan coast I've seen
Thee tow'ring on thy summit green;
So glowr the saints when first is given,
A fav'rite keek o' glore and heaven;
On earth nae mair they bend their ein,
But quick assume angelic mein;
So I on Fife wad glowr no more,
But gallop'd to Edina's shore.

FURTHER READING

William Dunbar, *The Poems of William Dunbar*, edited by James Kinsley, Oxford, Clarendon Press, 1979.

William Drummond of Hawthornden, *Poems and Prose*, edited by Robert H. MacDonald, Edinburgh, Scottish Academic Press, 1976.

Poems by Allan Ramsay and Robert Fergusson, edited by Alexander Manson Kinghorn and Alexander Law, Edinburgh, Scottish Academic Press, 1974.

Robert Burns, *Poems*, selected and edited by William Beattie and Henry W. Meikle, Harmondsworth, Penguin, many reprints.

Hugh MacDiarmid, *Complete Poems*, edited by Michael Grieve and W.R. Aitken, Harmondsworth, Penguin, 2 Volumes, 1985.

Robert Garioch, *Complete Poetical Works*, edited by Robin Fulton, Edinburgh, Macdonald Publishers, 1983.

Norman MacCaig, *Collected Poems*, London, Chatto & Windus/The Hogarth Press, 1985.

Sydney Goodsir Smith, *Collected Poems 1941-1975*, London, John Calder, 1975.

Donald Campbell, *Selected Poems 1970-1990*, Edinburgh, Galliard, 1990.

For other poets included in this anthology see any good catalogue such as that of The Scottish Poetry Library, Tweeddale Court, 14 High Street, Edinburgh.

The Oxford Book of Scottish Verse, chosen by John MacQueen and Tom Scott, Oxford, Oxford University Press, latest edition, 1989.

A Choice of Scottish Verse 1560-1660, by R.D.S. Jack, London, Hodder & Stoughton, 1978.

For anthologies of modern Scottish poetry the choice is wide.

Robert Fergusson 1750-1774: Essays by Various Hands to Commemorate the Bicentenary of his Birth, edited by Sydney Goodsir Smith, Edinburgh, Nelson, 1952.

Alexander Law, *Robert Fergusson and the Edinburgh of His Time*, Edinburgh, Edinburgh City Libraries, 1974.

Gordon Wright, *A Guide to the Royal Mile: Edinburgh's Historic Highway*, Edinburgh, Gordon Wright Publishing, 1986.

The Hon. Lord Cullen, *The Walls of Edinburgh: A Short Guide*, Edinburgh, The Cockburn Association, 1988.

Robert McNeil, *The Porteous Riot*, Edinburgh, Scotland's Cultural Heritage, 1987.

Roy M. Pinkerton and William J. Windram, *Mylne's Court. Three Hundred Years of Lawnmarket Heritage*, Edinburgh, University of Edinburgh Information Office, 1983.

David Daiches, *Edinburgh*, London, Hamish Hamilton, 1978.

E.F. Catford, *The Story of a City*, London, Hutchison, 1975.

J.F. Birrell, *An Edinburgh Alphabet*, Edinburgh, James Thin, The Mercat Press, 1980.

Trevor Royle, *The Story of Literary Edinburgh: Precipitous City*, Edinburgh, Mainstream, 1980.